Rowland Purton

DEAR GOD

Basil Blackwell · Publisher

First published 1984

Published by
Basil Blackwell Publisher
108 Cowley Road
Oxford OX4 1JF

British Library Cataloguing in Publication Data

Purton, Rowland W.
 Dear God
 1. Encyclopedias and dictionaries
 I. Title
 032'. 02   AE6

 ISBN 0–631–13203–1

Typeset in 11 on 12½ point Palatino by Freeman Graphic, Tonbridge
Printed in Great Britain

Contents

Acknowledgements

The author and publisher would like to express their appreciation to all who have given permission to reproduce copyright material.

(1) Extracts from *The Book of Common Prayer* of 1662, which is Crown Copyright in England, are reproduced by permission of Eyre & Spottiswoode London (91b, 134f, 193e, 201b, 206d). Some of the ancient prayers, for which original sources are indicated, may also be found in *The Book of Common Prayer*.

The following are reprinted by kind permission:

(2) The Bahá'í Publishing Trust (121c, 189).

(3) *Good News Bible* (36, 104bcd, 115a, 190a, 195cd, 202a, 203c) © American Bible Society 1976, published by the Bible Societies/Collins.

(4) Blandford Press: *Infant Teacher's Assembly Book* (13b, 60a, 198d); *Infant Teacher's Prayer Book* (13d, 16a, 20b, 68c, 96a, 146f); *Sing and Pray* (98bc).

(5) Church Missionary Society: *All our Days* ed. Irene Taylor and Phyllis Garlick (170a).

(6) Central Board of Finance of the Church of England: *In Excelsis* (CIO Publishing, 1962) (51a, 71d).

(7) Collins Publishers: *Short Prayers for the Long Day* by Giles and Melville Harcourt (73b, 172); *Prayers for Young People* by Dr. William Barclay (59e, 72e, 105b, 137ab, 201a).

(8) The Revd. A. Stanley J. Fisher (204b).

(9) Fount Paperbacks: *More Prayers for Young People* (65b), *More Prayers for the Plain Man* (167c) both by Dr. William Barclay.

(10) Miss Doris M. Gill: 'Come let us remember the joys of the town' v.5 (46c).

(11) Mrs. Mary Hedges: *With One Voice* Sid G. Hedges (39c, 105d, 120ef, 159a, 184de, 185ab, 196e, 200f).

(12) Hodder and Stoughton Ltd: *A Book of Childhood Prayers and Verses*, Carolyn Martin © W.I. Books Ltd (3a, 39a, 70c, 81d, 87e, 191d); *God Loves You*, Catherine Marshall (56d, 80a, 204c); *Prayers for Younger Children*, Brenda Holloway (96b); *Well God, here we are again* © J.A.C. Bryant and David Winter (44d, 62c, 71e, 119cd).

(13) The Revd. Richard G. Jones (54).

(14) Brother Kenneth CGA: *prayabout* by Brother Kenneth CGA and Heather Howell, published by CIO (2a, 80b); *Live &*

Pray by Brother Kenneth CGA and Sister Geraldine Dss CSA, published by CIO (91c).

(15) Lion Publishing: *Children's Prayers from Around the World* (122); *The Lion Book of Children's Prayers*, Mary Batchelor (133e).

(16) Lutterworth Press: *Prayers at Breakfast* (60d, 92a); *Prayers for all Seasons* (99b, 155a, 162a, 167b) both by Beryl Bye.

(17) Manchester University Press: Mary Boyce, *Sources for the Study of Zoroastrianism* (ed. Hinnells) 1984 (185e).

(18) Mayhew McCrimmon Publishers: *It's Me O Lord* (143b) and *The One Who Listens* (169b) by Michael Hollings and Etta Gullick.

(19) The Methodist Church, Division of Education and Youth: *School Hymn Book of the Methodist Church* (11b, 19d).

(20) Methodist Publishing House: *Methodist Hymn Book 1933* (10e).

(21) A.R. Mowbray & Co. Ltd: *God of All Things*, Joan Gale Thomas (157d).

(22) National Christian Education Council: (66d, 128a); *New Child Songs* (6a, 20a, 24c, 48a, 66a, 154d, 192d); *Prayers to use with 5–8s* (28d, 97a, 98a, 131b, 152a, 190d, 201c); *Prayers to use with 8–11s* (82b); *When you pray with 7–10s* (35a, 90e, 169a).

(23) The National Society (Church of England) for Promoting Religious Education: (72d, 76a); as publisher of *Hymns and Songs* (48b).

(24) Oxford University Press: *Enlarged Songs of Praise*, 'Lord of all hopefulness' v.1, (2f) by Jan Struther (1901–53); *Songs of Praise for Boys and Girls*, 'I love God's tiny creatures' v.2 (37) and (198f) both by G.W. Briggs (1875–1959); *Prayers and Hymns for Junior Schools* (71a, 105a, 199b); *The Daily Service* (68d, 124d, 160c).

(25) Marjorie Rose and Collins Educational: *The Morning Cockerel Hymn Book* (205c).

(26) Routledge & Kegan Paul Ltd: *Liberal Prayer Book* (121b).

(27) Scholastic Publications (Magazines) Ltd: A.W.L. Chitty, from *Child Education* (21a).

(28) Scripture Union Publishing: *Prayers for Children 1* (12a, 29a, 66b, 88f), *Prayers for Children 2* (94f, 97b, 129a, 157a, 165b) by Zinnia Bryan; *Praying for Family* (191b), *Praying for Friends* (91a), *Praying for School* (124e, 129d), *Praying for Special Days* (191c) by David Lewis.

(29) The Society for Promoting Christian Knowledge: *The Children's Service* comp. C.S. Woodward (121a).

(30) Union of Liberal & Progressive Synagogues: *Service of the Heart* (182d).

(31) United Synagogue, London: *Children's Siddur for Sabbaths and Festivals* (197abcd).

(32) The Headmaster, Uppingham School: *Prayers in use at Uppingham School* (199f).

(33) The Headmaster, Westminster School: *Westminster School Prayer Book* (73c).

(34) I have endeavoured, unsuccessfully, to trace and obtain permission from possible owners of copyright for some prayers and verses (10a, 20c, 125a, 156e, 170d, 181a, 200a).

(35) Prayers 39b, 45d and 174d are in *God of a Hundred Names*, arranged by Victor Gollancz and Barbara Greeve, published by Victor Gollancz; 2e in *Little One's Album* (McDougalls); 1 and 123 in *The Book of a Thousand Poems* (Bell & Hyman).

It will be appreciated that recourse has been made to a great many publications other than those mentioned above and some prayers have been memorised during a long period. Should any copyright have been unwittingly infringed, the author extends his sincere apologies and will gladly rectify the omission, if notified, in any future edition.

The author would also like to express his appreciation of the great amount of work and support given by his wife, Sylvia, in the production of this book.

Introduction

How often do we need help in wording a prayer for a special or unusual occasion? Or how often do we feel a need for a wider selection on everyday themes? This comprehensive book of over 900 prayers for children should meet both needs and its indexing will facilitate the finding of them. It will be invaluable in infant, junior and middle schools as well as in the hands of leaders of church, Sunday school and children's organisations.

In most sections the simpler prayers precede the more difficult but not always. It is recognised that often a simple prayer may be needed for older children and a 'difficult' one, perhaps adapted, may be just what is needed for the younger ones. With the exception of a few major themes, prayers on a given subject occupy a single page or a double spread, making selection possible almost at a glance.

Most of the prayers have been especially written for this book but some have been taken from other publications, the number following the prayer indicating the source (see page vi). Others marked * are traditional prayers or of source unknown. All prayers not indicated by either means or not attributed to any other author or source are the copyright of the author.

The use of capital letters for pronouns referring to God has not been standardised: in general the form found in the original publication has been used.

As the prayers may frequently be used in assemblies of children of various faiths, the concluding words 'For Jesus' sake' or 'Through Jesus Christ our Lord' have been omitted from original prayers, as has the 'Amen'. In many instances leaders will wish to add such words before the Amen.

If this book proves of value to teachers and leaders, and if it can help children in any way to meet with God, it will have achieved its purpose.

ROWLAND PURTON

DAYS AND SEASONS

Praise the Lord for all the seasons,
   Praise Him for the gentle spring,
Praise the Lord for glorious summer,
   Birds and beasts and everything.
Praise the Lord, Who sends the harvest,
   Praise Him for the winter snows,
Praise the Lord, all ye who love Him,
   Praise Him, for all things he knows.[35]

Mary Anderson

1

I can say it to my family, I can say it to my friends,
I can say it at school – so I'll say it to you –
Good morning, God, you're Great![14]

Dear Father God, thank you for this new day.
Help us to use it well.

Dear Father God, thank you for keeping us safely through the night, for waking us this morning and giving us a new day to enjoy. Help us today, in our work and in our play, to do and be the best we can.

Make us remember, O God, that every day is thy gift, and ought to be used according to thy command; through Jesus Christ.

Dr. Samuel Johnson

Thank you, God in Heaven
For a day begun.
Thank you for the breezes,
Thank you for the sun.
For this time of gladness,
For our work and play,
Thank you, God in Heaven
For another day.[35]

Lord of all hopefulness, Lord of all joy,
Whose trust, ever child-like, no cares could destroy,
Be there at our waking, and give us, we pray,
Your bliss in our hearts, Lord, at the break of the day.[24]

Jan Struther

O Almighty God, thank you for keeping us safe through the past night. Be with us through this day. Defend us from all sin, and harm. Help us to be obedient to our parents and teachers, kind and gentle to our companions. Make us honest in all we do, and true in all we say. Create in us a clean heart, and may thy Holy Spirit lead us in the way that we should go. For Jesus Christ's sake. [12]

As we start our new day, dear God, we offer our thanks
for every blessing received since last we came together:
    For the comfort and security of our homes;
    For the love of our parents and others;
    For the companionship of our special friends;
    For a peaceful night and restful sleep;
    For food and drink to make us strong;
    For books to read and games to enjoy;
    For radio, television and music.
For these, and all your gifts, we say 'Thank you, God'.

Grant us, O Lord, to pass this day in gladness and peace, without stumbling and without stain, that reaching the eventide victorious over all temptation, we may praise thee, the eternal God, who are blessed, and dost govern all things, world without end.

Mozarabic Liturgy

A Hindu prayer from the Rig Veda (c. 1500 BCE)

We praise you with our thoughts, O God;
We praise you as the sun praises you in the morning:
May we find joy in being your servants;
Keep us in your care,
Forgive us our sins,
And give us your love.

New Year

O God, a new year gives us the chance to make a fresh start. Forgive us for all that we did wrong in the old year and help us to do better in the new.

Dear Father God, a new year can mean a new start. Please help us to start 19 . . well and to do our best all through the year.

Dear God, we don't know what will be in store for us in the coming year but we do know that you will be near us always in our good times and our bad ones and that we can always talk to you about these. Thank you, dear God.

> Another year is dawning;
> Dear Master, let it be
> In working or in waiting,
> Another year for Thee.
>
> *Frances Ridley Havergal*

As we meet together for the first time in a new year, let us ask God for his guidance and blessing.
In all that we plan for the coming year,
> *Guide us and bless us, O God;*
As we seek not to make again the mistakes of the past,
> *Guide us and bless us, O God;*
In our resolutions to do only what is good and right,
> *Guide us and bless us, O God;*
As we look for new ways of helping others,
> *Guide us and bless us, O God;*
As we offer our lives to be used in your service,
> *Guide us and bless us, O God.*
>> For the sake of Jesus Christ our Lord.

Dear God, at the beginning of a new year we say thank you as we remember all the blessings that last year brought. Please help and guide us throughout the whole of this year so that *we* may enjoy the year . . . and others may enjoy us.

Dear God, help us to think of New Year
    as a new beginning,
    with new hopes
    and new opportunities
    to learn and do new things.
Give us, as we start our year,
    new thoughts of what our world should be,
    a new wish to make it a better place,
    new ideas as to how we can help others,
    and a new desire to serve you.
May we begin the year ready and willing to be of service
to others and to you in the strength that you give us.

Be with us, God, the whole year through.
When storm clouds loom or skies are blue,
Teach us, good Lord, to trust in you.

And I said to the man who stood at the gate of the year: 'Give me a light that I may tread safely into the unknown!'
    And he replied:
'Go out into the darkness and put thine hand into the Hand of God. That shall be to thee better than light and safer than a known way.'
    So I went forth and finding the Hand of God trod gladly into the night.

M. L. Haskins

EPIPHANY (*see under 'Christmas' p. 31*)

We thank You, loving Father God,
For things which warm us so;
For glowing fires and woolly gloves
Which make cold fingers glow;
For winter clothes and games to play
When we can skip and run . . .
And thank you for our cosy beds
When winter's day is done.[22]

Hilda Rostron

Dear Father God, thank you for flowers and berries and all other beautiful things which brighten the dark winter days.

When cold north winds blow
Or there's ice and snow;
When skies that are grey
Spread gloom through the day;
Dear Father, above,
Fill us with your love;
Give brightness and cheer
Because you are near.

Thank you, dear God, for things to enjoy in winter:
For snow and snowballs and snowmen;
For games to play in the ice and snow;
For blazing fires and hot drinks;
And for warm homes to go home to: Thank you, God.

Dear Father God, today we are thinking about the birds in winter that are unable to find food or shelter. Thank you for caring people who put out food for them. Show us how we can help them too.

Thank you, dear God, for the wonders of winter:
Glistening frost on trees and plants;
Patterns made by Jack Frost on the window panes;
Carpets of pure white snow;
Icicles that hang from the gutters;
Bright red berries and evergreen trees.
Thank you for being such a great God and for giving us such a wonderful world.

When the weather is cold, we say thank you, God, for our cosy homes, our warm school, and the warmth within us that comes from the love of those around us.

We thank you, God our Father
For the season of winter and the things we can enjoy,
Thank you, God our Father;
For beautiful things, like snowflakes, icicles and frost patterns on the window panes,
Thank you, God our Father;
For the fun we can have with snowmen, slides, snowballs and sledges,
Thank you, God our Father;
For warm clothing, blazing fires, cosy homes and lots of interesting things to do indoors,
Thank you, God our Father.
As we say thank you for all these things, help us to remember those who are unable to see the beautiful things, those for whom snow and ice bring hardship and those who have little comfort in their homes. Show us how we can help them and, as we think of them, make us more ready to count our blessings.

Thank you, dear God, for the first signs of spring, which add brightness to winter's gloom: and thank you for your love which brings brightness even to our darkest days.

Shrovetide and Lent

Dear God, at this time people in many lands are enjoying all the fun of carnival before the season of Lent begins. Teach us the art of enjoying ourselves with others, sharing fun and festivity as we do things together and knowing that the more we put into such things the more enjoyment we shall get out of them.

Dear God, today is Pancake Day and we are looking forward to eating ours. We remember that people used to eat pancakes to use up food they could not have during Lent to help them remember Jesus for forty days before Easter. Today we do not stop eating these foods but we ask you to help us to think, during the coming season of Lent, about Jesus and all he did for us, and to be thankful.

Prayers for Ash Wednesday
Dear God, help us as we prepare ourselves for Easter. We are sorry for all the wrong things that we have done and we humbly ask that you will forgive us. Then, knowing that our sins are forgiven, may we know you better and understand the great love that was shown at Eastertide.

Dear Father God, today we ask your forgiveness for all our unkind words and deeds and for anything that has hurt someone or that you see is wrong. Please help us to do better.

> Teach me, O God, to take a good look at myself,
> To see what is good about me and what is not so good,
> To thank you for the good things
> And to ask your forgiveness for the bad things,
> So that, with your help, I can grow
> To be all that you would wish me to be.

Dear Father God, we remember how Jesus was tempted to do wrong things but refused to do so. Help us to follow his example and turn aside from anything we know to be wrong.

Keep us in your care, O God, and when we are tempted to do wrong help us not to do it.

At this time of year, dear God, help us to remember how Jesus gave up his life for us on the cross. Make us ready to give up something we like as a reminder to us of what happened so long ago for us.

Dear God, we remember how Jesus spent forty days in the wilderness to find out how you wanted him to do your work. Help us, as we grow, to find out what you want *us* to do.

> Lord Jesus Christ,
> You know what it is like to be tempted
> For you were tempted in the wilderness;
> You know how easy it is to do wrong things
> And much harder to do things the right way;
> You know, too, what it is to be disappointed,
> To be misunderstood,
> To be let down by friends,
> To be cruelly treated and put to death,
> Yet able to forgive those who wronged you.
> Please help us
> Not to give in when we are tempted,
> Nor to be hurt by what others do.
> Forgive us if in any way we have wronged you;
> Help us to forgive those who wrong us;
> And help us to follow your example.

Spring

We thank Thee for the springtime, Lord,
  For birds and trees and flowers,
For running brooks and humming bee,
  For sunny, happy hours.[34]

Frances Weld Danielson

Thank you, dear Father God, for all the brightness of spring-time, for spring flowers and catkins, for new life in the countryside and on the farm, and for the bright sunshine and blue sky. Help us to remember that you have given these and so many other lovely things, and help us always to remember to say thank you.

Dear Father God, open my eyes to see all the beauties of spring and keep me thankful for all your gifts to me.

Now the spring is here and the dark winter days are behind us, we say thank you, God, for watching over us and we ask for health and strength so that we can enjoy your world.

O Lord of every lovely thing,
  The maker of them all,
Who from the winter's gloomy wing
Doth shed the splendours of the spring,
  On Thy great name we call.

With flowers that through the valleys teach
  Thy love and truth divine,
With streams that sing, and hills that preach,
With waves that laugh on every beach,
  We praise Thee we are Thine.[20]

Robert Wilfrid Callin

The spring again is here,
Life wakes from winter's gloom;
In field and forest far and near
Sweet opening flowerets bloom.

Lord, touch our careless eyes;
New life, new ardour bring,
That we may read Thy mysteries,
The wonder of Thy spring.

Arthur Christopher Benson

In this prayer the children respond by saying the words printed in italics.

Let us praise God for his gift of spring, the time of new life and new beginnings:
Praise ye, praise ye, God the Lord.
For warm sunshine, blue sky, fleecy clouds, and longer brighter days:
Praise ye, praise ye, God the Lord.
For fresh spring showers filling the streams and rivers, cleansing the streets and hedgerows:
Praise ye, praise ye, God the Lord.
For the coming of the birds and their joyous songs, the colour and scent of flowers, the new green of bush and tree:
Praise ye, praise ye, God the Lord.
For the blustering winds, strong and free, bringing health to all:
Praise ye, praise ye, God the Lord.
For all young life in field and farm:
Praise ye, praise ye, God the Lord.
For new-turned earth, ready by man's care for the sowing of seed.
Praise ye, praise ye, God the Lord.
O God, open our eyes that with heart and mind we may enjoy the beauty of thy world. We are glad that we belong to thy world. By thy help may we enter into its glory and increase its joy.[19]

Lord Jesus, make me like the man who lent You his donkey –
happy to lend to others.[28]

Zinnia Bryan

At the beginning of Holy Week we come to you, O God, and
ask that you will help us to understand those things which
happened in this week so long ago.

We think of the great joy when Jesus rode into Jerusalem on
a donkey and people shouted their praises.

We think of the anger of Jesus at the trading in the Temple
and how the leaders plotted to get rid of him.

We remember the last supper Jesus shared with his friends,
who all let him down before the night was out.

We think of the sad events of the trial of Jesus and his death
on the cross and we rejoice in his rising again at Easter. For this
week we praise your name, O God.

Prayers for Maundy Thursday
O Lord Jesus Christ, who commanded your disciples to love
one another, help us to do just that and so show that we can be
your disciples.

We remember, dear God, how Jesus was betrayed by one
whom he had counted amongst his friends and followers. Help
us today never to let him down by doing anything that is
wrong or hurtful.

Dear God, we remember how Peter, when he was afraid, said
that he did not know Jesus and how sorry he was afterwards
that he had let Jesus down. Give us courage when we are afraid
of what others may say or do, and make us always ready to
stand up for what we know to be right.

Prayers for Good Friday
Dear Father God, we cannot fully understand all that happened on Good Friday but we believe that Jesus died so that we could be forgiven and call you Father.

Dear Loving Father, we are thinking this morning of Jesus Christ, who died on a cross. We are very sorry that this happened to Him, and we want very much not to hurt Him any more. Help us to love Him and stand up for Him, and to do what He wants us to do, all our lives. We ask it for His sake.[4]

Easter prayers

Jesus died;
Jesus rose again;
Jesus lives.
Praise be to you, O God.

Thank You, God, for Easter joy,
Meant for every girl and boy.
Jesus rose at Eastertide –
Now He's always at our side.[4]

Quietly, dear God, we think of all those things that happened in that week before the first Easter Sunday – the betrayal, trial and death of Jesus and all the sadness of those events.
(Pause in silence for a while)
But Easter comes as a time of real happiness when we remind ourselves how Jesus rose again from the dead, showed himself to his disciples and changed their sadness to great joy.
So we join with Christian people of all the ages since then as we shout and sing for joy:
'Christ is risen, Hallelujah – praise be to you, O God'.

Rogationtide and Ascension

Rogationtide, the days preceding Ascension Day, is the time for asking God's blessing on the growing crops and giving thanks for the earth's resources.

We offer our grateful thanks, dear God,
    For all the fruits of the earth, our daily food;
    For all the resources of materials and power;
    And for the rich harvests of the sea.
Hear our prayers
    That we may use all your gifts wisely;
    That we may not waste or misuse anything you have given;
    And that you will show us how to use these gifts for the benefit of all mankind.

On Ascension Day
On this day, dear God, we remember how Jesus returned to you after telling his followers to carry on his work. Thank you for Jesus and for his followers who have done as he told them. Help us to learn the ways of Jesus and then work faithfully for him.

        Thank you, God:
        That Jesus came to us;
        That he died for our sins;
        That he rose again;
        That he returned to you;
        And that he lives in the hearts
        of all who love him.

Dear God, we cannot really understand how Jesus rose again from the dead, how he appeared to his disciples and then, after forty days, returned to you. But we remember how he said he would return to his Father and prepare a way for us and so we ask that you will help us to come to you believing all that Jesus promised.

Whitsun and Trinity

Dear God, we remember how you promised to send your Holy Spirit into the lives of those who ask. May your Holy Spirit come into us, helping us to understand your ways and guiding us through life's journey.

> Holy Spirit, help us
> Daily, by Thy might,
> What is wrong to conquer,
> And to choose the right.
> *William Henry Parker*

> Spirit of love, make us loving;
> Spirit of truth, teach what is right;
> Spirit of wisdom, give us understanding;
> Spirit of power, grant us your strength;
> Spirit of God be with us,
> Within us and around us,
> To fill us and inspire us.

A prayer for Trinity
Dear God, help us to learn of you and to get to know what you are like:

God the Father, creator of the world and all that is in it, who made man in his own likeness;

God the Son, Jesus Christ, who showed us the way to live and died so that our sins could be forgiven;

God the Holy Spirit, who comes into the lives of all who ask, to give us heavenly wisdom and guidance.

And so, to you, God, the Father, the Son and the Holy Spirit, be all honour and glory now and for ever.

Further prayers: WHITSUN p. 176; TRINITY pp. 174, 194, 203, 206

> Praise to God for summer days,
> For summer clothes and summer plays,
> And for our summer holidays.[4]

Dear Father God, thank you for the summer sunshine, the warm breezes and long days. Help us to enjoy summertime in your world.

Dear Father God, the warm days of summer give us a chance to explore the outdoor world and enjoy the world of nature. Thank you for so much that is lovely and interesting. Open our eyes and ears to the beauty of the world.

We think today, dear God, of people who cannot enjoy the summer as we can – the blind, the old, the sick and the housebound. Show us how we can share our enjoyment with them.

> Praise be to you, O God, for summertime:
> For warm sunshine and cool breezes,
> *Praise be to you, O God;*
> For long evenings when we can play outdoors,
> *Praise be to you, O God;*
> For sports and games to enjoy with others,
> *Praise be to you, O God;*
> For picnics, outings and holidays,
> *Praise be to you, O God;*
> For a whole world of nature to explore,
> *Praise be to you, O God;*
> For family and friends who share our enjoyment,
> *Praise be to you, O God;*
> For all of these and for so many other blessings,
> *Praise be to you, O God.*

For air and sunshine, pure and sweet,
   We thank our heavenly Father;
For grass that grows beneath our feet,
   We thank our heavenly Father;
For lovely flowers and blossoms gay,
For trees and woods in bright array,
For birds that sing in joyful lay,
   We thank our heavenly Father.

Anon.

Ask children what they enjoy seeing in summer.
O God, there are so many lovely things to see in summer:
        Pretty flowers
        Butterflies
        Tall leafy trees
        . . . . (etc.)
Help us to remember that these are all part of your creation and your gifts to us. Thank you, God, for all the joys of summer.

Dear God, help us this summer to enjoy our world – the mountains and hills, rivers and streams, fields and forests, moors and glens, lakes and ponds. As we look at these, give us a sense of wonder at your creation – a beautiful world which we must not spoil.

Dear God, there is so much to be enjoyed in summer:
We enjoy the warm days and the long evenings;
We like the colour of the flowers in our gardens
And the flowers that grow in fields and hedgerows;
We enjoy watching the birds and many small creatures;
We have fun playing outdoors with our friends;
We like our outings to the sea or the country
And especially going away for our holidays.
Thank you, God, for summer days.

During the summer, O God, we enjoy playing games with our friends. Help us to play fairly so that all can enjoy the games. And, if we lose, please help us to be good losers.

> All things praise you, Lord most high,
> Birds and beasts – so why not I?

Thank you, dear God, for all the outdoor activities we can enjoy in summer-time.

For things we can do on our own or with friends – walking, and cycling, lazing in the sun or playing games;

For family outings to places of interest, for picnics in the country and special excursions;

For colourful outdoor entertainments by Morris dancers, bands and others who enjoy themselves by giving pleasure;

For carnivals and fairs, where we enjoy the processions, the colour, the noise, the music and the amusements.

For holidays in this country and abroad, when we can see new places and things and meet different people;

For these and so much else to do on fine, warm days, we give you thanks, dear God.

> For flowers that bloom about our feet;
> For tender grass, so fresh, so sweet;
> For song of bird, and hum of bee;
> For all things fair we hear and see,
> Father in heaven, we thank Thee!
>
> For blue of stream and blue of sky;
> For pleasant shade of branches high;
> For fragrant air and cooling breeze;
> For beauty of the blooming trees,
> Father in heaven, we thank Thee!

Ralph Waldo Emerson

As the sun warms the world in summer, dear God, may the sunshine of your love bring warmth into our hearts and enable us to spread brightness wherever we may go.

O God, it's going to be very hot today;
I shan't feel much like doing my work;
I shall be too hot and sticky
And perhaps sleepy, too.
But some people will be worse off than I am –
People who do dirty work under the blazing sun
And those who work at furnaces.
I shall be better off than they are today
So help me count my blessings and enjoy my day.

Dear God, it is nearly time for us to have our summer holiday when we can go on outings to the seaside or the country. Help us to enjoy this lovely time of the year in ways that will not hurt or annoy other people.

Let us pray:
For shady trees and green grass, for flowers in garden and hedgerow:
Thanks and praise to Thee, O Lord.
For happy times with our friends, for expeditions to river and sea, for picnics among the hills and on the moors:
Thanks and praise to Thee, O Lord.
For sunbathing and swimming and cycling, for jolly walks and sports:
Thanks and praise to Thee, O Lord.
Heavenly Father, help us, as we share the joys of summertime, to remember those who cannot enjoy it to the full – the deaf, the crippled, the blind, those living in sunless streets or working in crowded places, the very old. May we pass on other joys to them.[19]

Harvest

First the seed
And then the grain;
Thank you, God,
For sun and rain.

First the flour
And then the bread;
Thank you, God,
That we are fed.

Thank you God,
For all Your care;
Help us all
To share and share.[22]

Lilian Cox

For juicy apple, plum, and pear,
For all the farmer's work and care,
For food when all the fields are bare,
We thank You, heavenly Father.[4]

For the golden corn, for the apples on the tree,
For the golden butter and the honey for our tea,
For fruit and nuts and berries, that grow beside the way,
We praise thy loving kindness Lord, and thank thee every
day.[34]

Elizabeth Gould

For the harvest of land and sea, thank you, God.

Blessed art thou, O Lord our God, King of the universe, who
bringest forth bread from the earth.

A Jewish blessing

Bread is a lovely thing to eat –
God bless the barley and the wheat;
A lovely thing to breathe is air –
God bless the sunshine everywhere;
The earth's a lovely place to know –
God bless the folks that come and go!
Alive's a lovely thing to be –
Giver of life – we say – bless thee![27]

A.W.L. Chitty

Thank you, dear God, for the harvest safely gathered in, food for people and for animals – and thank you for all the people who helped to provide this harvest.

Dear Father God, we have brought all sorts of interesting things for our Harvest Service – apples, oranges, tins of fruit, packets of biscuits, tea, eggs, sugar . . . (*add other foods on display*) – because we want to say 'Thank you' for all your gifts of food and for all who have worked so that we might have them. [Bless the people to whom these gifts will be taken and make us glad that we have been able to help them.]

Dear Father God, we thank you for the harvest and all your gifts of food. We think of .... (*mention some on display*) and thank you for seeing that we do not go hungry.

Dear God, please teach us
To be thankful for all the good food we have;
To be thoughtful for those who have very little;
To remember that harvests should be shared;
To be careful not to waste good food;
And to thank all who help us to have it.

21

Today, dear God, we have lots of good things to eat. Thank you for our food and for all who work so that we may have it.

For the golden harvest, ripe fruits and so much else you have given us, praise be to you, O God.

> Dear God,
> Please fill our stomachs with food,
> Our minds with thankfulness
> And our hearts with love.

Dear Father God, thank you for all the mouth-watering fruit and not-so-interesting vegetables that we can buy in the shops to make us grow big and strong. And thank you for those who grew them so that we could buy them.

> Today, dear Father God, we think of harvest time and we say thank you as we praise you for your goodness.
> For fields of golden grain for bread, cakes and biscuits,
> *We praise your Name, dear God;*
> For potatoes, carrots and food that grows in the ground,
> *We praise your Name, dear God;*
> For apples, cherries and plums in the orchards,
> *We praise your Name, dear God;*
> For oranges, bananas and fruits from overseas,
> *We praise your Name, dear God;*
> For tea and coffee and other things to drink,
> *We praise your Name, dear God;*
> For sugar and spice and all things nice,
> *We praise your Name, dear God;*
> And for ordinary things like cool fresh water,
> *We praise your Name, dear God.*

For the harvest safely gathered in we say, 'Thank you, God.'

Thank you, dear God, for the harvest of the sea, the many kinds of fish we can eat, caught by fishermen far out at sea, crabs and lobsters and many kinds of shellfish found near the coast. Thank you for so much to eat, and thank you for the fishermen who go out, often in bad weather and rough seas, so that we can enjoy our fish.

Dear Father God, thank you for that harvest that comes to us all the year round, the harvest provided by the cows and the dairy farmers who look after them, a harvest of milk, cream, butter, cheese, yoghurt and other milk foods that help us to grow strong. Thank you for all who work so hard to produce these things and for people like milkmen who work in all kinds of weather to bring them to our homes.

We thank you, dear God, for all those people who have helped to give us our harvest:
For farmers who planted and reaped the crops,
Thank you, God our Father;
For people in other lands who grew different foods for us,
Thank you, God our Father;
For sailors who brought the food from overseas,
Thank you, God our Father;
For workers in docks and factories,
Thank you, God our Father;
For millers and bakers, packers and canners,
Thank you, God our Father;
For market salesmen, shopkeepers and delivery men,
Thank you, God our Father;
And for parents who earned the money to buy all this good food we enjoy,
Thank you, God our Father.

Autumn

Dear Father God, we thank you for all the beauties of autumn, for the lovely colours of the trees and the bright red berries. Thank you for this time of the year. Help us to enjoy it.

Thank you, dear God, for fruits, nuts and berries – food for our friends the animals and birds. Thank you for your care for them and for us.

> Autumn leaves are falling down,
> Leaves of red and gold and brown,
> Fluttering, fluttering, fluttering down.
>
> Birds are flying overseas,
> Seeking warmer lands than these;
> Flying, flying overseas.
>
> Hedgehogs want their winter sleep,
> Seek a hole both warm and deep,
> Snuggle, snuggle down to sleep.
>
> God provides for winter care
> Of his creatures everywhere;
> Thank you, God, for winter care.[22]
>
> *E. M. Stockham*

Dear Father God, now that summer has passed and the evenings are getting chilly, we say thank you for our cosy homes, our warm clothes and those who have provided them for us.

> For all the joys of autumn
> We give you thanks, O Lord.

Children make a response in this prayer with the phrase in italics.

For this season of autumn,
    We thank you, God our Father;
For pale sunshine and misty mornings,
    We thank you, God our Father;
For ripening fruits and bright red berries,
    We thank you, God our Father;
For falling leaves that rustle as we walk,
    We thank you, God our Father;
For colourful leaves and autumn flowers,
    We thank you, God our Father;
For animals and birds preparing for winter,
    We thank you, God our Father;
For these and all your blessings;
    We thank you, God our Father.

O God, our Father, the misty mornings, falling leaves and smoky bonfires remind us that winter days draw near. Thank you for all we enjoyed this summer: help us to remember the happy times.

In this season of acorns and conkers we think of all the fun we can have with them – making things and playing games. We remember, too, that some provide food for animals and that others will grow into great trees. How wonderful is your creation, O God – you thought of everything.

O God our Father, help us to see beauty in the world around us; the fruits and berries of woodland and hedgerow; the fruit of the orchard and the fields of golden corn; the beautiful colours of trees and falling leaves; and the glow of autumn sunshine after misty mornings. For these and all your blessings we praise your name, O God.

Hallowtide

Thank you, God, for the fun we have at Hallowe'en with punkies and parties. We remember how people used to fear evil things on this night and we thank you that we no longer do so. But hear our prayer, O God, for any who do.

Dear God, on this day when we think of all sorts of evil and strange things, we say thank you that we can just enjoy the fun of the day without being afraid as people used to be. And for any who are afraid of such things, we ask that they may know that your power is greater than any other, and so place their trust in you.

> *An old Scottish prayer:*
> From ghoulies and ghosties and long leggety beasties
> And things that go bump in the night,
> Good Lord, deliver us.*

A prayer for All Saints' Day
Today, O God, we remember all the saints through the ages who have lived courageously and served you and their fellows faithfully, some facing persecution and death because of their beliefs. Help us to follow their example and have the courage to stand up for all we believe to be right.

A prayer for All Souls' Day
Today, dear God, we remember the millions of ordinary people who have never made a name for themselves as saints but who have lived good lives and remained faithful to you. We do not expect to be remembered in history but we ask that we may be counted amongst those who have lived good lives and been true to their God.

Advent

Help us to remember, in this season, O God, how Jesus came to be the Light of the World. Help us to live as he taught and so help to spread light ourselves.

During this season of Advent, dear God, help us to remember
How Jesus came into the world;
How he said he would come again;
How he comes into the hearts of all who love him.
Help us to make room in our hearts for Jesus to come to us today.

Today, dear God, we remember how the prophets foretold that the Messiah would come, how John the Baptist came to prepare the way for him and how his birth was announced to his mother, Mary. Thank you, God, that all came to pass just as you said it would.

Dear God, in Advent, as we light our candles, we remember Jesus, who came long ago to bring light into the world. Thank you for sending Jesus to teach us of your love.

Dear God, it is a long time since Jesus came to be the Light of the World but he said he would come again and he comes into the hearts of all who want him to. As we look forward to his birthday, show us how to open our hearts so that he can come in and make our lives the brighter.

Dear God, just as one light brings brightness to a dark room, so Jesus brought light to a dark world. Help us to follow him so that our many lights will help to sweep away the darkness in the world of today.

Christmas

Dear Father God, help us to have a happy Christmas, and help us to make it a happy Christmas for other people too.

Dear God, we say a big 'Thank you' for everything we are going to enjoy this Christmas but especially for Jesus, your Son, whose birthday we shall remember on Christmas Day. Thank you for all you have given us.

At Christmas time we say, 'Thank you, God.'
For pretty lights, Christmas trees and decorations,
Thank you God;
For Christmas dinner, Christmas pudding and mince pies,
Thank you God;
For Father Christmas, presents, toys and parties,
Thank you, God;
For Christmas cards, carols and entertainment,
Thank you, God;
But especially for sending Jesus to us,
Thank you, God.

For all our fun and happiness,
For all that's bright and gay,
Thank you, thank you, thank you, God,
This joyful Christmas Day.

For Mary and Joseph watching
Baby Jesus in the hay,
Thank you, thank you, thank you, God,
This joyful Christmas Day.

For the shepherds told by angels
Where the baby Jesus lay,
Thank you, thank you, thank you, God,
This joyful Christmas Day.[22]

Lord Jesus, I would hate it if my friends were so busy enjoying themselves and opening presents of their own on my birthday, that they forgot all about me. Please help me not to do that to You.[28]

Zinnia Bryan

Dear God, thank you for all we enjoy at Christmas:
    Christmas trees and fairy lights;
    Christmas crackers, decorations and candles;
    Christmas dinner and Christmas pudding;
    Christmas cake and mince pies;
    Christmas parties with family and friends;
    Christmas presents to give and receive;
    Father Christmas filling our stockings;
    Christmas cards to greet our friends;
    Christmas carols and the Christmas story – reminding
    us how you sent Jesus.
Thank you, God, for your love in sending Jesus to us and for all we enjoy because he came.

O Lord Jesus, when you came into the world there was no room for you in the inn and you were born in a stable. Teach us to make room for you to come into our hearts – and into the best part, not the part that is left when we have made room for other things first.

As we look forward to Christmas with all its fun, feasting, decorations and the giving of presents, help us to remember, O God, that we have Christmas because you loved the world so much that you sent your Son, Jesus, to come and live amongst people and show them how to know you as their Heavenly Father. As we give and receive our gifts, help us to remember your great gift to us and, in return, offer to you the gift you most desire, our loving hearts.

Dear God, as the angels proclaimed the birth of Jesus as 'tidings of great joy to all people', help us to pass on to others the joy that is in our hearts, so that Christmas may be a time of happiness and goodwill.

Before this prayer, invite children to say what they will enjoy this Christmas, then offer the prayer with the response 'Praise be to you, O God.'

For Christmas trees, fairy lights and decorations,
   Praise be to you, O God;
For turkey, Christmas pudding, and ....
   Praise be to you, O God;
For the presents we give and those we receive,
   Praise be to you, O God;
For ....
   Praise be to you, O God.

Dear Father God, today we remember those people who will be lonely this Christmas, those who will have no family parties and those who will not enjoy good food. We say thank you for people who will spend their Christmas in helping others and we ask that we may do what *we* can to bring Christmas cheer to someone who needs it.

O Holy Child of Bethlehem,
Descend to us we pray;
Cast out our sin, and enter in;
Be born in us today.
We hear the Christmas angels
The great glad tidings tell;
O come to us, abide with us,
Our Lord Immanuel.

Phillips Brooks

Although associated with Christmas, the coming of the wise men is more correctly celebrated at Epiphany (6th January) and the following prayers could equally well be used for either occasion.

Thank you, God, for the story of the wise men and the gifts they offered to Jesus. Help us to offer him our best gifts too.

Invite the children to say what gifts they think could be offered to God

Dear God, you have made us like we are and have given us all sorts of gifts. Help us now to offer them to you, so that they may be used wisely.
We bring our hands, that they may be of help to others
    Accept our gift to you, O God;
We bring . . . our minds . . . work in school . . . hearts . . .
(*and any other suggestions from children, each with the above response*).
Dear God, take our offerings and grant us your blessing.

O Lord Jesus Christ, to whom wise men of old brought their gifts, help us to bring to you our best gifts, the gifts of ourselves and our talents to be used in your service.

Dear God, we remember how you led the wise men to Jesus and how they presented their costly gifts. We ask that you will lead us to find Jesus and help us to know what gifts we can give. May we offer whatever special abilities we have so that they may be used in your service and for the benefit of others in your name.

End of the year

As we come to the end of 19 . ., dear God, we say a big thank you for all we have enjoyed and for your help when we have had problems. Please be with us still as we start the new year.

As we come to the end of the year, dear God, we think of the year that has passed and of some of the things that have been important to us.
   (*Pause*)
We think of special things we have done in school.
   (*Pause*)
We think of happy times with our families.
   (*Pause*)
We think of holidays, outings and special treats.
   (*Pause*)
We think of people who have meant a lot to us.
   (*Pause*)
Thank you, dear God, for many happy memories and for all that this year has meant to us.

At the end of the year, O God, we have many memories:
   Happy times with our family and friends;
   Many lessons learned in and out of school;
   Games we have played and holidays enjoyed;
   The enjoyment of our pets and our hobbies . . .
There are so many things that we cannot recount them all, but for all the many blessings we say, 'Thank you, God.'

Dear Father God, we can think of lots of happy times in 19 . . and we say thank you for them. We can think of many mistakes we made in 19 . . and we are sorry. We can think of many lessons learned in 19 . . and we ask that we may remember them. May we learn from the lessons of 19 . . so that we may not make the same mistakes again and that next year will be a time of even greater happiness than this year has been.

Special days

Prayers for St. George's Day

Dear God, we think on this day of one who was brave and noble, fighting that which was evil in his day. Help us to fight the dragons of this world and to live in such a way that we may be an example to others. Help us so to live that evil may be set aside and we play our part in making this England the kind of land that you would have it to be.

> Bring me my bow of burning gold!
> Bring me my arrows of desire!
> Bring me my spear! O clouds, unfold!
> Bring me my chariot of fire!
> I will not cease from mental fight,
> Nor shall my sword sleep in my hand,
> Till we have built Jerusalem
> In England's green and pleasant land.
>
> *William Blake*

A prayer for St. David's Day

Dear God, as St. David (Dewi) of old faithfully worked for you to spread the work of your kingdom, and as people through the years have sounded your praises in great cathedrals or chapels in the valleys, so grant that we may do what we can to make this land of our fathers a land of peace and happiness as we rejoice in all your goodness towards us.

A prayer for St. Andrew's Day

Dear God, let your blessing today rest upon the land of Scotland and its peoples, its great cities and its lonely crofts, its highlands and its islands, its mountains and moorlands, rivers and lochs. As we think of St. Andrew, who forsook all to follow Jesus, may we offer ourselves to your service so that, as we follow your teachings, we may help to build for a better future.

A prayer for St. Patrick's Day
Dear God, today we remember the one who stood firm before the king and was not afraid to say what he believed. In this day, when there is so much that seems to be wrong, help us to follow his example and work for the day when all shall follow in your ways and live with love in their hearts for all your people.

On St. Valentine's Day
Thank you, dear God, for the fun of sending valentines but even more for the joy of having someone to love. Today we are happy for all people who themselves are happy because they love one another.

A prayer for All Fools' Day
Today, O God, as we think of making fools of others, guard us from all foolishness of word or deed that would hurt others and from the foolishness of forgetting you.

A prayer for Michaelmas (St. Michael and all angels)
Almighty God, we thank you for all your power and might, and for the protection against evil which you give to all who trust in you. Help us by your heavenly powers to overcome all the evils in the world around us.

For use on a Saint's Day
Dear God, today we remember St. ...., who heard your call and willingly spent *his* life in your service, helping others in *his* time, by *his* teaching and example, to grow nearer to you. Help us, this day, to follow *his* example and serve you faithfully in whatever task you call us to, in the name of Jesus Christ.

Bonfire Night
　　　　For all the fun of bonfire night,
　　　　For fireworks lighting up the sky,
　　　　For catherine wheels and sparklers bright,
　　　　And rockets shooting way up high,
　　　　　Thank you, God our Father.
　　　　For hot-dogs, toffee apples, pop,
　　　　And roast potatoes in the fire,
　　　　For jumping jacks that skip and hop,
　　　　And smoke-gold flames that leap up higher,
　　　　　Thank you, God our Father.[22]

Dear Father God, we know how easy it is to have accidents with bonfires and fireworks. As we enjoy ourselves tonight, please help us to be careful so that we are not hurt.

Remembrance Day
Dear Father God, many people are sad today when they think about friends and loved ones killed in war. Comfort them, we ask, and teach people how to live together in peace.

On this day, dear God, we keep silence as we remember people who died while serving their country, those who have been very seriously disabled, and all who suffer as a result of war and fighting.

(*Pause after each sentence*)
　　　　Hear our prayer for all who mourn.
　　　　Comfort all who suffer and help the disabled.
　　　　Bless all who have to care for the suffering.
　　　　Help all who have hatred in their hearts.
　　　　Forgive us that we have not learned to live in peace.
　　　　Teach us to think of all people as brothers and sisters.
　　　　Give wisdom to all who have authority in the world.
　　　　Guide the nations of the world into the ways of peace.
　　　　And help us all to live in love toward our neighbours.

From the book of Ecclesiastes in the Old Testament come these thoughts about times and seasons.

Everything that happens in this world happens at the
time God chooses.
He sets the time for birth and the time for death,
the time for planting and the time for pulling up,
the time for killing and the time for healing,
the time for tearing down and the time for building.
He sets the time for sorrow and the time for joy,
the time for mourning and the time for dancing,
the time for making love and the time for not making love,
the time for kissing and the time for not kissing.
He sets the time for finding and the time for losing,
the time for saving and the time for throwing away,
the time for tearing and the time for mending,
the time for silence and the time for talk.
He sets the time for love and the time for hate,
the time for war and the time for peace.[3]

Ecclesiastes 3: 1–8

To God, in whose hands are all our days, be all praise and glory.

THE WORLD AROUND US

Dear Father, who hast all things made,
And carest for them all,
There's none too great for Thy great love,
Nor anything too small:
If thou canst spend such tender care
On things that grow so wild,
How wonderful Thy love must be
For me, Thy loving child.[24]

G. W. Briggs

Thank you, dear God, for this great big world which you have made and for all the wonderful creatures and things that you have put into it. Help us always to take care of your world.

>All things bright and beautiful,
>All creatures great and small,
>All things wise and wonderful,
>The Lord God made them all.

Open our eyes, O God, to the wonders of the world you have made; and open our lips to sing your praises.

Dear Father God, we say thank you for the lovely world which you have made and especially our own land with its cities, towns, villages and open country. Thank you for farms and fields, trees and flowers, animals and birds, sea and sky . . . and so much else. For all these things we thank you, God.

>Lord, make me see your glory in every place.
>
>*Michelangelo*

>Dear God,
>Thank you for putting us in your world
>And for giving us so much to enjoy:
>Thank you for the sun by day and moon by night;
>For fleecy clouds in the bright blue sky;
>For fields of grass and shady trees;
>For singing birds and buzzing bees;
>For lots of creatures great and small;
>For people, families and friends;
>For food and clothes and homes and schools
>And blessings more than we can count . . .
>Dear God . . . Thank you.

Thank you God for guide-dogs,
And pets both big and small,
For elephants and kangaroos,
And snowflakes as they fall,
For little things like bumble-bees
And birds and butterflies,
And big big things like mountains,
And lovely starlit skies.
For funny things like penguins,
And ducks that quack aloud,
And clever things like tiny ants
All scurrying in a crowd.
For mums and dads and family,
And days spent by the sea,
And circus clowns, and birthday cakes,
Oh! thank you God for me![12]

M. Copp

O heavenly Father, protect and bless all things that have breath: guard them from all evil and let them sleep in peace.[35]

Albert Schweitzer when a child

We worship God (*Ahura Mazda*) who created the cattle, and the waters, and the wholesome plants.[11]

A Zoroastrian prayer from the Zend-Avesta

For the beauty of the earth,
For the beauty of the skies,
For the love which from our birth
Over and around us lies:
Father, unto Thee we raise
This our sacrifice of praise.

F. S. Pierpoint

God make my life a little flower
That giveth joy to all,
Content to bloom in native bower,
Although the place be small.

Matilda Betham-Edwards

Dear Father God, thank you for all the beautiful flowers that we can enjoy in parks and gardens, in hanging baskets and window boxes and for all the pleasure they give.

The response after each sentence: 'Thank you, God'.
For all the lovely flowers that grow in our gardens;
For wild flowers of the countryside;
For flowers in greenhouses or in our homes;
For the blossom of bushes and trees;
For trees of many shapes and colours.

As the sun shines through the trees to bring some brightness to the dark forest, grant, O God, that the sunshine of your love will never fail to reach into the darkest places of this world.

For pink and white blossom adorning the trees;
For many wild flowers that bloom by the roadside;
For woods full of bluebells and fields with red poppies;
For deep purple heather on mountain and moorland;
For beautiful flowers we grow in the garden;
For bushes of roses and shrubs with fine flowers;
For vases of flowers and plants in our houses;
For flowers we send to say 'Greetings' or 'Thank you',
For so much beauty
We praise you, O God.

As the trees are firmly rooted in the soil, reaching their branches toward the heavens and their leaves toward the sunlight, grant, O Heavenly Father, that we may be rooted in your ways and, reaching out toward you, find the sunshine of your love, so that we, too, become strong with good firm foundations for life.

Dear Father God, who feeds and waters the trees so that they grow strong to provide shelter for man and homes for the animals, nourish us, we pray, that we may also grow in strength until we can be of good use to others.

Dear Father God, please make me like the flowers – content to grow just where they are, making the most of even the poorest soil, yet bringing colour, brightness and pleasure to all who see them.

Dear God, may the mighty trees, which have stood firm for hundreds of years against gales and storms, inspire us to stand firm against all the storms and perils of this life in the strength which comes from the power of our mighty God.

Thank you, dear God, for the forests and woodlands where we can enjoy the peace and quietness broken only by the scurrying of animals, the sound of the birds and the rustling of leaves beneath our feet. Thank you for the trees that give us shade and provide homes for so many wild creatures. Thank you for small clearings where the sun lends its brightness. And thank you for the wonder that comes to us as we remember that this is all part of your creation.

Animals and birds

Dear Father God, we thank you for all the animals, birds and other wild creatures that we enjoy seeing. Help us never to harm them but remember that you have made them all and put them in our world.

Dear Father God, you have made so many different kinds of animal:

> Large ones like elephants
> . . . . . and small ones like mice;
> Fierce ones like tigers
> . . . . . and gentle ones like rabbits;
> Some we can see in the country
> . . . . . and some we can see only in zoos;
> Some that work for us
> . . . . . and some we keep as pets.

Thank you for them all.

> I like animals, dear God.
> I like to watch them
> And I like to hold them.
> I like all sorts of animals . . .
> Help me to be kind to them
> So that they like me.

> Let us think about animals . . . (*Pause*)
>   Those we have as pets and companions . . . (*Pause*)
>   Guide dogs and others that help people . . . (*Pause*)
>   Animals that work for us . . . (*Pause*)
>   All animals on the farm . . . (*Pause*)
>   Wild animals of the countryside . . . (*Pause*)
>   The larger animals in zoos and parks . . . (*Pause*)
>   . . . (*any that may be of especial interest*) . . . (*Pause*)
> Thank you, dear God, for all the animals that share our world.

All things which live below the sky,
    Or move within the sea,
Are creatures of the Lord most high,
    And brothers unto me.

Almighty Father, King of Kings,
    The lover of the meek,
Make me a friend of helpless things,
    Defender of the weak.

Edward John Brailsford

Ask children what kind of birds they would like to think about and incorporate these in the prayer.
    Thank you, O God, for the birds we enjoy:
        Robins that perch on the garden spade;
        Song birds that sing their praise at dawn;
        Noisy seagulls around the harbour;
        Owls which hoot at night;
        Swallows skimming the river on summer evenings;
        Pigeons that circle overhead;
        Hens in the farmyard;
        . . . add (or substitute for above) children's suggestions.
    Thank you, God, for so many birds in our world.

Dear Father God, we remember how Jesus told us that you know and care about the sparrows. Help us always to remember that you care for us; and help us, in turn, to care for all your creatures.

Dear God, it is fun in spring to watch the birds building their nests, laying eggs and hatching tiny baby birds. Help us never to touch the nests, the eggs or the babies, nor to do anything that would frighten the birds during this time.

Pets and working animals

Thank you, dear God, for animals and birds that we can keep as pets – dogs, cats, rabbits, guinea-pigs, hamsters, gerbils, budgerigars, canaries and some more unusual ones. Help us to look after those that are in our care for they depend so much upon us.

Dear Father God, thank you for our pets and all the pleasure they give us. Help us to be kind towards them always.

Dear God, we want to say thank you for our pets: for the pleasure and companionship they give us.
Thank you, too, for animals that work for us or help to provide our daily needs:
    Horses that pull carts and those we ride;
    Sheepdogs that help the shepherds with their work;
    Guide dogs that are the eyes of blind people;
    Police dogs and guard dogs to protect property;
    Cows and goats that give us milk;
    Elephants, camels and oxen in other lands.
Thank you, God, for these and all our animal friends.

Thank you, Lord, for animals, – the big ones that run wild, and the ones we have as pets. Help us to be kind and gentle with our cats, dogs, hamsters, budgies and other pets, and to look after them carefully.

We ask you to bless the Royal Society for the Prevention of Cruelty to Animals in all it does to protect and care for helpless animals. Through Jesus Christ our Lord. [12]

Thank you, dear God, for guide dogs for blind people, for those who train them and for those who raise money so that blind people can have their own special guide and companion.

Dear Father God, we enjoy having our pets but sometimes we have smaller creatures too that we like to look after:

> Caterpillars of many kinds
> Stick insects or silkworms
> Frogs, toads or newts
> Snakes or lizards
> Fish in an aquarium
> Worms in a wormery
> Bees in a beehive
> . . . (*any others kept by children or in school*).

Thank you, God, for such little things. Help us to treat them well.

Dear God, thank you for our pets and thank you for all those people who care for them when they are sick or injured – veterinary surgeons and members of organisations such as the PDSA and RSPCA. Bless those people in their work of caring for those creatures which are unable to look after themselves.

Dear Father God, thank you for horses. They are such friendly animals and give people so much help and pleasure – horses that work, horses to ride, horses for racing and ponies for children. Help us to look after any that are in our care.

Hear our humble prayer, O God, for our friends the animals, Thy creatures. We pray especially for all that are suffering in any way; for the overworked and the underfed, the hunted, lost or hungry; for all in captivity or ill-treated, and for those that must be put to death.

We entreat for them Thy mercy and pity; and for those who deal with them we ask a heart of compassion, gentle hands and kindly words.

Make us all to be true friends to animals and so more worthy followers of our merciful Saviour, Jesus Christ.[35]

Dear God, our city is such a busy and exciting place with lots and lots of people. Yet in the city there are some people who are very lonely. Please help them.

> Dear God, this is *our* town.
> We think of its busy streets;
> The cars and lorries, buses and bicycles;
> The shops and the market;
> Offices and public buildings;
> Churches and chapels.
> We think of parks and gardens
> With trees and flowers;
> Of birds and all wild creatures.
> We think of thousands of people,
> In many kinds of home . . .
> And much more besides.
> Dear God, this is *our* town;
> Please help us to keep it nice.

We thank Thee, O God, for the numberless things
And friends and adventures which every day brings,
O may we not rest until all that we see
In towns and in cities is pleasing to Thee.[10]

Doris M. Gill

Dear Father God, thank you for our town:
    For the buildings and streets we know so well;
    For so many people who live and work here;
    For cars and vans, buses and trains;
    For trees and flowers to brighten the streets;
    For the birds that cheer us with their singing;
    And for all wild creatures that also live here.
Open our eyes and ears to the sights and sounds around us and teach us how to enjoy our town.

Dear God, thank you for this village and all the people who live and work here. Thank you for the countryside with its fields and woods and hedgerows. Thank you for the birds and wild creatures that also live here. It is only a small part of your big world but it is *our* part and we say thank you for all it means to us.

Dear God, thank you for our part of the country:
For........................ (*Include anything of beauty or*
For........................ *worthy of particular mention*
For........................ *in the locality.*)
For all of these, and the pleasure of living in this part of the country, we give you thanks, dear God.

Dear God, please help us, whenever we are in the country, to observe the Country Code and leave the countryside unspoiled for others.

Thank you, O God, for this beautiful land:
For mountains and hills, highlands and lowlands,
 Thank you, O God;
For dales and valleys, fells and glens,
 Thank you, O God;
For open moorland and hills of purple heather,
 Thank you, O God;
For lakes, lochs and llyns, rivers and rushing streams,
 Thank you, O God;
For rocky coastlines and islands large or small,
 Thank you, O God;
For forests of mighty trees and orchards pink with blossom,
 Thank you, O God;
For fields of growing crops and lush green pastures,
 Thank you, O God;
For National Parks, where people can enjoy such beauty,
 Thank you, O God.

Thank you, God, for lovely sea,
Rippling waves come splashing me;
Cooling water washing toes,
In it comes and out it goes.

Thank you, God, for shining sand,
Tiny grains slip through my hand;
Can you think what I will build
When I get my bucket filled?

Thank you, God, for open air;
How I like to stand and stare,
Watching boats go sailing by,
Listening to the sea-gulls cry.

Thank you, God, for every day;
I can run and I can play,
Many things to do and see.
Thank you, God, for making me.[22]

John Dean

Thank you for the big blue sea,
For the sands, so wide and free.
For the shells, and rocky pool,
For the sea winds, blowing cool;

For my bucket and my spade,
And the castles I have made,
Shining gulls, and sparkling foam,
And my treasures carried home.[23]

Dear God, thank you for all the fun we have by the sea,
For the beach, spades, buckets and sandcastles;
For rock pools, crabs, seagulls and fish;
For boats, amusements, ice-cream and swimming;
For so much to enjoy, thank you, God.

Water

Dear Father God, thank you for the pure, fresh water that we have to drink; thank you for those who learned how to make it safe to drink; and thank you for those who supply it to our homes.

Thank you, Heavenly Father, for water:
For the cool refreshing water we drink,
   Thank you, Heavenly Father;
For plenty of water for cleaning and cooking,
   Thank you, Heavenly Father;
For water for washing and water for bathing,
   Thank you, Heavenly Father;
For fun in the water, for swimming and splashing,
   Thank you, Heavenly Father;
For morning dew and falling rain,
   Thank you, Heavenly Father;
For lakes and ponds, rivers and seas,
   Thank you, Heavenly Father;
As we say thank you, please keep us mindful of people in other lands who have very little. Bless all who help to find water in very dry lands.

Dear God, we can have such a lot of fun with water and it is so useful as well. Thank you for providing us with water and with plenty of it.

Thank you, dear God, for rivers and streams, lakes, ponds and the wide open sea. May we do nothing to spoil them.

Dear God, thank you for fun in the water when on holiday or an outing. Help us to enjoy ourselves but to take special care not to get into danger or cause worry to others.

Care and conservation

Dear Father God, we thank you for all that is beautiful in the world. Teach us to do nothing that would spoil it for others.

Sometimes, dear Father God, I see a lovely flower that I would like to pick and take home . . . but then no one else would be able to enjoy seeing it. Help me not to be selfish but to think of others and to do nothing to take away their enjoyment of our lovely world.

Dear Father God, give me a love of all the small creatures of the world – even those I do not like; and help me to care for them, for you made them all.

Dear Father God, there are lots of beautiful things in our world and we thank you for giving them to us. There are also many ugly things and ways in which people have spoiled the world. Please help us to keep our world beautiful and to do nothing that would spoil it.

Ask children what things they have seen which spoil the neighbour-hood, the countryside or the world.
Dear God, there are so many things which people have done to spoil your world. We think of litter and .... and .... Please help us to do nothing to spoil it for others.

Dear God, I like lots of the animals and birds – but there are some things I *don't* like, such as spiders, wasps, earwigs and snakes. Help me to remember that you made them all and just because *I* do not like them that is no reason for harming them.

Heavenly Father, Maker of the world in which we live, give us a love of the countryside, its lanes and fields, its woods and streams, and open spaces; and let us keep it clean from litter and unspoilt for those who shall come after us, through Jesus Christ our Lord.[6]

H. W. Dobson

Thank you, dear God, for so much in the world to see, to hear and to enjoy:
> the beauties of the fields and open spaces;
> the colours of blossom and shade of trees;
> the many wild creatures large and small;
> the songs and flight of birds;
> the strange creatures of sea and shore;
> the hum of insect sounds in summer.

Help us to enjoy all that is around us and to do nothing to harm any part of your creation.

Dear God, if we go fishing with our nets in a pond we find all sorts of interesting creatures. Help us to enjoy looking at them but to remember to put them back as they are all needed for life in their pond-world.

Dear God, we enjoy the flowers and trees that make our world beautiful and we are sorry that some children pull up the flowers or damage the trees. Help us to take care of things that grow, and please prevent us at all times from being destructive.

Dear Father God, you have given us a wonderful world. Please help us to look after it and teach us never to be cruel or unkind to even the smallest of your creatures.

The weather

Dear God, a lovely sunny morning like this makes us feel good! Thank you for the sunshine that warms us and brightens our day and for the sunshine of your love to warm and brighten our lives.

Dear God, I don't like it when the lightning flashes and there are crashes of thunder. Sometimes it scares me and so I ask you to be near to me at times like these to make me brave and unafraid.

Dear God, we got very excited this morning when we looked out and saw the snow, and we had lots of fun on our way to school with snowballs.

But it isn't much fun for old people, so perhaps we can do things for them.

And it isn't much fun for birds, which cannot find food and depend upon us to feed them.

Please help us to share our joy by being helpful.

When the ground is icy, dear God, please help us not to fall and hurt ourselves. Be with old people and others who find it difficult to walk.

Dear God, when it is foggy it can be very frightening because we cannot see. Please be with us as we travel and keep us from harm.

Dear Father God, help us not to be afraid on foggy days but to be extra careful. Please take care of us, for you can see everything, even when we cannot.

Dear God, on a dull morning like this, when the sky is hidden behind the clouds, brighten our day with the knowledge that you cannot be hidden from us and then help us to brighten the lives of others.

Dear God, we do not like the rain very much:
    We get very wet sometimes on our way to school;
    We cannot go out to play our games;
    Sometimes it leaks into our homes or our school;
    And sometimes it causes floods.
But we know that we need the rain:
    We need it to make our crops grow;
    We need it to provide water for drinking and cooking
    . . . for washing and many other things.
We also remember what happens in lands where the rain does not fall, where there are no harvests, no food and nothing to drink except for water from wells.
    So we say thank you, God, for the rain.

Dear God, on days like this, when strong winds blow, we close our doors and windows to keep it out. We cannot see the wind but we can see what it does and we can feel it. You are like that – we cannot see you but we know that you are about. Help us never to shut you out of our lives.

        Whether the weather be cold,
        Or whether the weather be hot;
        Whether the weather be dry,
        Or whether the weather be not;
        We'll weather the weather,
        Whatever the weather,
        Whether we like it or not.
Teach us, good Lord, that we need all kinds of weather and to be content with the bad weather as well as the good.

God of concrete, God of steel,
God of piston and of wheel,
God of pylon, God of steam,
God of girder and of beam,
God of atom, God of mine,
All the world of power is thine!

Lord of cable, Lord of rail,
Lord of motorway and mail,
Lord of rocket, Lord of flight,
Lord of soaring satellite,
Lord of lightning's livid line,
All the world of speed is thine!

Lord of science, Lord of art,
God of map and graph and chart,
Lord of physics and research,
Word of Bible, Faith of Church,
Lord of sequence and design,
All the world of truth is thine!

God whose glory fills the earth,
Gave the universe its birth,
Loosed the Christ with Easter's might,
Saves the world from evil's blight,
Claims mankind by grace divine,
ALL THE WORLD OF LOVE IS THINE![13]

Richard G. Jones

OUR OWN WORLD

Dear God . . .

There are so many people who make up *my* world:
  My family and friends;
  My teachers and helpers;
  My neighbours and lots of others.

There is so much to enjoy in *my* world:
  My work and play;
  My games and pastimes;
  My home and my food . . .

As I grow, help me to learn to use all my abilities not just for myself but to give help and pleasure to others.

Us

Dear God, we say thank you for making us in such a wonderful way with eyes and ears, hands and feet, minds and hearts that all work together in a way that we cannot understand. Help us to take care of our bodies.

Hands to work
And feet to run,
Helping me
Have lots of fun;
Ears to hear
And eyes to see,
These are gifts
You've given me.
Let my mouth
Sing out your praise
Now and all
My earthly days
Let my heart
Be filled with love,
Father God
In heaven above.

Dear Father God, you made me like I am, so please help me to be the sort of person you would like me to be.

I want to do
What I want,
But then I find
I don't always like
what I want.
I guess, God,
You'd better
straighten me out.[12]

Catherine Marshall

Your love, dear God,
Is higher than the sky above,
Deeper than the earth beneath,
And reaches further than we can see.
Thank you, God,
That we are right in the middle of it.

Dear God,
You have given me eyes to see the beauties of our world;
You have given me ears to hear its many different sounds;
You have given me a nose to catch all lovely scents;
And a mouth with which to praise my God for all of this.
Please let me never forget to do so.

O God, help me to remember that my face tells people what
kind of person I am. Help me to be a cheerful person with a
happy smile that spreads sunshine wherever I go.

Dear God, we are an odd lot
But that is how you made us
And we can *all* call you 'Father'.
Thank you, Father, for making us as we are.

Dear God, you have given me a tongue which can help or hurt:
Please help me to control it.
    May it be used to speak words of comfort and cheer;
    Always used kindly, thoughtfully and wisely:
    May it never be sharp or hurtful, lying or boastful,
    Upsetting other people or causing trouble.
Teach me, dear God, when I should speak and when it is better
not to do so . . . and when I *do* speak, please give me wisdom to
choose my words aright.

Home

Dear Father God, thank you for my home and my family who share it with me. Please show me how to be kind and helpful to everyone in my home.

Dear Lord Jesus, you know what it was like to live in a home with your family. Please help me to make my home as happy as you must have made yours.

Thank you, God our Father, for our homes and all the pleasures we enjoy in them.
> For a place where we can live with our family,
>> *Thank you, God our Father;*
> For a family who all help to make our house a home,
>> *Thank you, God our Father;*
> For our own rooms and comfortable beds,
>> *Thank you, God our Father;*
> For books and toys and games to enjoy,
>> *Thank you, God our Father;*
> For good food and someone to cook it for us,
>> *Thank you, God our Father;*
> For our own little piece of garden to look after,
>> *Thank you, God our Father;*
> For all of this and so much more that home means to us,
>> *Thank you, God our Father.*

Dear Father God, when visitors come to our home, please help us to make them feel 'at home' by giving them a warm welcome and helping them to be at ease with us.

Dear Father God, as we thank you for our homes, we remember people in many places who have no home. Please bless them and all the people who are trying to help them.

Dear God, I want to say thank you for my own room at home where I can keep all my bits and pieces. It is nice to know that it is my special part. Please help me to keep it tidy. And please help me, too, to look after the other parts of my home, which I share with the rest of the family.

Thank you, God, for all the love and care which our parents have put into our homes to make them the kind of place where all the family can love and care for each other. Help us also to show love and care so that home can be a happy place for us all.

Dear God, forgive us if sometimes we are not content and envy people who have a bigger or more comfortable home than we have. Help us to remember many people who have less than we have and then try to make our home as happy and comfortable as we can.

Thank you, dear God, for home:
    For the comfort and warmth and love that is there;
    For all the people with whom we share it;
    For our own rooms and things we can call 'ours'.
Teach us to show our thanks
    By sharing in the responsibility of looking after it;
    By not being selfish, bad-tempered or thoughtless;
    By helping others in whatever way we can.
So may home be a happy place in which we show our love for one another and where friends and visitors always feel welcome.

Help me never to use my home simply for my own convenience, but to be a real partner in it, and to try to put into it more than I take out.[7]

Dr. William Barclay

Family

Dear God, we thank Thee for our families; for fathers and mothers, brothers and sisters. Help us to be kind and loving in our homes, so that we make other people glad.[4]

Dear Father God, thank you for my family and all that they mean to me. Help us always to be happy together.

Thank you, dear God, for those who mean so much to us – our family who love us and care for us. It is good to be a member of a family and especially a happy one, so we ask that you will help us to do all we can to make ours a happy family.

Dear Father, who in your love has set us in a family: give us a real love and concern for the well-being of one another.[16]

Beryl Bye

Thank you, God, for Mum.
She's *my* Mum
And she means so much to me.

Thank you, dear God, for our mothers, helping us and caring for us, doing so many things in our homes and looking after our daily needs. Teach us how we can show our thanks by doing little things that will help them – and please help us to remember to say thank you.

Thank you, dear God, for our mothers and fathers and all they do for us. Help us to be helpful to them.

Thank you, dear God, for mothers. They do so much for us, feeding us, clothing us, looking after us and loving us – and so often we forget even to say thank you. Help us to try to do better in future, to be more thoughtful, more helpful and more thankful – better sons and daughters than we have been.

Dear Father God, it is good to have a father.
He is so strong and can do so many things.
He works to earn the money that our family needs.
He does all sorts of jobs around the home.
He helps us when we are tired or troubled.
He takes us out sometimes and plays with us.
And he does lots of other things too.
Thank you, God, for fathers.

Thank you, God, for grandparents. They do spoil us by giving us all sorts of things when they come to see us and we look forward to their visits to our home and the times when we go to see them. As they grow older, please be with them and keep them in your care.

As we come to you now, O God, we remember those of our family who are not here but at home or at work. Please bless them all and help them through the day.

Dear God, we know that we should obey our parents and do what they want us to do in our home. But sometimes we are not good children: we grumble or whine when we are asked to do things and we find all sorts of excuses for not doing as we are told. Teach us, dear God, to be obedient at home and not show off or make a fuss when we have to do things that we do not wish to do.

Dear God, thank you for brothers and sisters. Sometimes we squabble and sometimes we are not very nice to each other but it is good to have them around and we ask you to help us to get on well together.

Lord Jesus, there are times when we wish we didn't have brothers or sisters:
    The older ones try to boss us around
    And younger ones sometimes annoy us;
    Sometimes they want the things that *we* want,
    And there are things that we have to share.
But there are other times when we are very pleased that they are there:
    We can do lots of things together;
    We can have fun and play games;
    We can care for and help each other.
You know what it was like in your home in Nazareth to be part of a family.
    Please help us to be good members of our families,
    To be kind, generous and considerate
    And to love one another.

Thank you, heavenly Father, for the new babies in some of our families. They look so tiny and helpless, and need so much done for them.[12]

Dear Father God, thank you for new babies and all the happiness they bring to a home. Bless them all and help their mothers and fathers, brothers and sisters to look after them.

Dear Father God, there is a new baby in ....'s family.
Please help them all to enjoy *him* and love *him*.

Dear Father God, we have lots of relations – parents, brothers, sisters, grandparents, uncles, aunts, cousins and others too. Some live with us: others we do not often see. But we are all one family and we ask you to bless us all, especially any who may need special help.

Dear God, today we are thinking of members of our family who live in a land far away. We are not able to see them but we can think of them and we ask that you will be with them.

Dear God, there are some members of our family that we do not get on with easily, especially those who are old.
Some are deaf and cannot hear what we are saying;
Some do not like the noise we make and get cross;
Some are rather crotchety and have funny ways;
Some no longer have any patience with children.
But they are part of our family and we know that one day *we* shall be old. Please help us to be patient with them and to try to be helpful even if it is difficult for us to do so.

Dear God, what an interesting family you have:
They speak different languages;
They are of many different colours;
And they call you by different names.
Help us to love all our 'brothers and sisters'
In countries all over the world.

Dear Father God, we think of all that a good father does for his family and we remember that you have told us to call you 'Father'. Thank you for being our Father. Help us to remember that we are part of your great world-wide family and to do what we can to be good children in that family.

Friends and neighbours

Dear Father God, thank you for my friends. It is nice to have good friends to play with and to work with. Help me to be a good friend to others.

Dear God, we have lots of people we call our friends. Thank you for them all and for the fun we have together.

Thank you, dear God, for friends:
Friends we can talk to and play with;
Friends who are interested in what we are doing;
Friends who stand by us when we have trouble;
And for Jesus, the best friend of all.

Some people, O God, do not seem to have any real friends. Perhaps it is because they cannot make friends easily, or because they are more interested in themselves or speak unkindly, or are spiteful or do nasty things. Help me to try to be friendly toward children who are like this even if I find it difficult.

Dear God, I have lots of people living near me and they are all different. Some of them I like better than others but they are all my neighbours. Make me kind to all my neighbours and especially those I find it difficult to like.

Friend of the children, who always art near,
Holding Thy hand I have nothing to fear.
Guided and guarded by Thee I would be;
No other friend is so precious to me.

Edith Greeves

Dear God,
Thank you for friends and all that we can do together;
Thank you for all the fun and games we enjoy;
Thank you for our special friends –
The ones we think of as good friends that we can rely upon.
Help us to be good friends too
So that others can rely upon us
And know that we won't let them down.
But please help us, too,
To be friends with those we do not like so much:
They need friends just as we do
And we know you would like us to be friends with them.

I thank you for my friends,
For those who understand me better than I understand myself,
For those who know me at my worst and still like me,
For those who have forgiven me when I had no right to expect
to be forgiven.
Help me to be as true to my friends as I would wish them to be
to me.[9]

Dr. William Barclay

> Help us, O God, to be *good* friends –
> Not out to get what we can from others
> But to give them what we can of ourselves.

Dear God, you know all about the people who live near us and
we think of as our neighbours.

Some of them are very helpful to us and some of them need
us to help them.

Some of them are very kind, cheerful and very nice to speak
to; some always seem miserable and crotchety.

Give us patience with those who are not nice to us and help
us to be kind and considerate to *all* our neighbours.

Birthdays

Happy, happy birthday!
Happy year begun!
God, who gives us birthdays,
Knows them every one;
God is kind and loving,
He is sure to hear;
So we ask His blessing
For another year.[22]

Florence Hoatson

Lord Jesus, today is ....'s Birthday. Thank You for looking after him/her during the past year, and keep him/her safe in the year to come. Please give him/her a happy day, and help us to do our best to make it happy, too.[28]

Zinnia Bryan

Dear God,
Thank you for my birthday.
Thank you for your love and care
Throughout the past year.
Please help me now
To grow up strong and healthy,
And ready to love others as you love me.

Comes a birthday once again,
Happy day, oh, happy day!
Through the sunshine, through the rain,
God has brought us on our way.

Father, let the new year be
Bright and holy, sweet and true;
Keep, oh, keep us close to Thee,
Day by day our whole life through.[22]

Frederick Arthur Jackson

Dear God, as we enjoy our birthdays
Help us to remember the blessings each year brings –
The love of parents, the comfort of home,
Our food, clothing and many other gifts.
Thank you for all your love and kindness.
Help me to use the new year you give me
To grow wiser, to work and study better
And to live happily with others for your sake.

Thank you, dear God, for all the fun of birthdays:
For waking up and knowing we are now a year older;
For the many birthday presents we receive;
For birthday cakes with lighted candles;
For birthday cards and 'Happy birthday' greetings;
For parties to enjoy with our family and friends;
For happy, happy birthdays, thank you, dear God.

Dear Father God, today is the birthday of .... (*and*
........................). We have wished *them* a 'Happy Birthday'. Now
we ask that you will help *them* to enjoy today and bless *them*
through their year.

Dear Father God, birthdays are such happy times with cards,
presents, parties and cakes with candles to blow out. Today is
the birthday of .... (*and* ....). Please help
them today to have a birthday that is a happy one to remember
and be with *them* through the coming year.

In our assembly today, O God, we have been remembering the
birthday of .... who became a very important person
in history because of .... Thank you for all *he* did
during his lifetime and for the example which *he* gave. Help us
so to grow that we, too, may have something worthwhile to
offer to the world.

Illness

Sometimes, dear Father God, we feel very miserable because we have a cold or some other illness. Thank you for all those who take care of us then to help us to get better.

> Dear God,
> Some of our friends are ill
> And are not able to come to school.
> Some of them have .... (*epidemic*);
> Some may feel fed up with themselves
> And others may be in pain.
> Please be near to all these friends
> And help those who look after them.
> Please make them well soon
> So that we can be together again.

O God, *we* come to You for help. Take care of .... who is ill (sick). Show the doctors what will help *him* most. Let the nurses who take care of *him* be kind and gentle and skillful. Let those who are anxious about *him* be brave and strong and unafraid. Give *him* courage when the pain hurts, and help *him* to get better.[4]

Lord Jesus, who for our sakes wast once a little child, and didst show Thy love for children by taking them up into Thine arms and blessing them: we ask Thee to bless those who are sick (*and especially* ....). Thy love toward them is greater than ours can ever be; therefore, O Lord, we trust them to Thy care and keeping.[24]

Dear God, at this time, when so many people are ill, we remember all doctors who have so much extra work to do and ask that you will give them the strength they need.

Death

Dear Father God, we are always sad when we hear that someone has died, and especially anyone who we know. [Today we think of ....] Be with all who are sad at this time and comfort them in their sorrow.

Dear God, ... has died and we are very sorry. Now *he* has gone to be with you and we thank you for our happy memories of *him*. Bless *his* family and comfort them in their sadness.

Dear Father God, we are thinking of those people who this day are mourning the loss of a member of their family or someone they loved. Please be very close to them, comfort them and strengthen them in their time of great sadness.

Dear God, you have taught us that when someone dies it is not just the end of life but the beginning of a new one. We feel sad because .... has died but we know that *he* is with you now. We ask that you will take away the sadness from all those who loved *him* and comfort them in their sorrow.

Dear Father God, today we are thinking of .... who has died. *He* has not been well for a long time and has had a lot of pain. Now *his* pain is over and *he* is with you so we say thank you for all our happy memories of *him* and we ask you to comfort *his* family at this time.

On the death of a famous person
Dear God, people in many places today are sad because .... has died (*been killed*). Thank you for all he did for (our country and) the world during his lifetime.

Learning and growing

Dear Father God, we are very small and we have so many things to learn as we grow up. Help us to remember what people tell us so that we can learn all we can. And help us to learn all we can of you so that we can grow up to be the kind of people that you would wish us to be.

Teacher of children, so wise and so kind,
O may I ever thy words keep in mind;
Learning of thee as I grow day by day,
Doing thy will as a little child may.

Edith Greeves

Help me to work
Help me to play,
Help me to learn a bit each day.

Teach me to wash,
Teach me to scrub,
To hang my clothes
To clean the tub.
To put my toys upon the shelf,
Teach me O Lord to help myself.[12]

M. Lee

Jesus, Friend of little children,
Be a friend to me,
Take my hand and ever keep me
Close to thee.

Teach me how to grow in goodness
Daily as I grow.
Thou hast been a child, and surely
Thou dost know.

Walter J. Mathams

Shine upon our hearts, O Lord, as the sun shines upon the trees, and as they spread forth their branches to the light, so may we open our hearts to Thy love, and grow in strength and goodness.[24]

Dear God, sow the seeds of your love in our hearts and help us so to grow that the beauty of your love may be seen in our lives.

> Teach me, Lord Jesus, as I grow,
> The things that you would have me know.

Lord Jesus, loving and helpful at home and at school
Help me to be like You.
Lord Jesus, growing up vigorous and strong
Help me to be like You.
Lord Jesus, working with a will in the carpenter's shop
Help me to be like You.
Lord Jesus, loving the flowers and the birds, the hills and the open sky
Help me to be like You.
Lord Jesus, a friend to everyone
Help me to be like You.[6]

H. W. Dobson

Heavenly Father, you know how we look forward to growing up. Help us, though, to make the most of being young, and prepare ourselves sensibly and patiently for the time when we shall have to earn our living and be parents and teachers ourselves. As we grow in size and in years, may we also grow in our understanding of you and of your ways with us. For Jesus Christ's sake.[12]

Health and faculties

Dear Father God, please teach me how to look after myself so that I can grow up fit and well – and make me thankful for all who help me to do so.

Dear Father God, I know it is important for my health that I should wash often and clean my teeth. Please help me to remember to do these things.

Dear God, please help me to keep my body healthy, my mind clean and my body pure for your sake.

> Praise to God for things we see,
> The growing flower, the waving tree,
> Our mother's face, the bright blue sky,
> Where birds and clouds go floating by;
> Praise to God for seeing.
>
> Praise to God for things we hear,
> The voices of our playmates dear,
> The merry bells, the song of birds,
> Stories and tunes and kindly words;
> Praise to God for hearing.[23]

Maria Matilda Penstone

O God, you have given me life, and I know that you want me to make something worthwhile out of it.
Help me
   To keep my body fit;
   To keep my mind keen;
   To keep my thoughts pure;
   To keep my words clean and true.
This I ask for Jesus' sake.[7]

Dr. William Barclay

Thank you, dear God, for our health and strength.
Teach us the importance of cleanliness
And the value of exercise
To keep us fit for life's duties and opportunities.
Teach us also to keep our minds and our thoughts clean
So that we may have a healthy attitude to life
As befits those who would be children of God.

Holy God, who madest me
And all things else to worship thee;
Keep me fit in mind and heart,
Body and soul to take my part,
Fit to stand, fit to run,
Fit for sorrow, fit for fun;
Fit to work and fit to play,
Fit to face life day by day;
Holy God, who madest me,
Make me fit to worship thee.[7]

Giver of all good things, we thank thee, for health and vigour, for the air that gives the breath of life, the sun that warms us, and the good food that makes us strong; for happy homes and for the friends we love; for all that makes it good to live. Make us thankful and eager to repay, by cheerfulness and kindliness, and by a readiness to help others. Freely we have received; let us freely give, in the name of him who gave his life for us.[33]

Bishop Thomas Ken

Dear God, please help me to look after myself so that I remain healthy in body and mind. Guard me against any habits or actions which could endanger my health and against dirty or unpleasant things which could make my thoughts impure or my words offensive.

Holidays and outings

Dear God,
Thank you for the holidays we can enjoy at the seaside:
there are so many lovely things to do.
We can swim or paddle or splash about in the water;
We can play games on the beach with bats and balls;
We can dig in the sand and build sandcastles;
We can look for shells, pebbles or seaweed;
We can find rock pools and starfish and crabs;
We can sit on the beach and watch the waves come in;
We can watch the fishing boats going into harbour;
We can eat ice-cream and drink cool fizzy drinks;
We can enjoy the shops, the amusements and the pier.
Thank you, God, for holidays
And especially holidays by the sea.

Dear Father God,
Thank you for holidays away from home –
Holidays by the sea or in the country,
And holidays in far away places.
Thank you for people who arrange them,
For those who take us there,
And those who make us comfortable
In our holiday homes.
Thank you, most of all,
For our parents,
Who pay for them and come with us,
So that we can do so many lovely things
Together as a family.

Dear God, we are looking forward to our holidays and we are
getting very excited about going away for a while.

Please help us to enjoy ourselves while we are away and to
discover new and interesting things.

We think of other children who will not be able to have a nice
holiday this year and we are sorry that they cannot go away.
Please be with those who are very disappointed.

Dear God, thank you for all the opportunities we have today to travel by road or rail, sea or air to far-away places. There are so many interesting things to see and do. Please help us to make the most of these holidays to find out about other places and the people who live in them.

Dear God,
We enjoy our holidays from school and especially those days when our parents have a holiday from work as well, the Bank Holidays and other special days when most people have a day off. It is nice to be able to go out as a family to an interesting place, a fair, a show, a circus, or some special event that has been arranged because it is a public holiday. Thank you for our family outings. And thank you for those people who have to work on public holidays – the bus and train drivers, the entertainers, and all others who help us to have a good day.

Dear God,
We do enjoy a day at the zoo so that we can see all those interesting animals:
Magnificent lions, tigers and other big cats;
Tall giraffes and beautiful deer;
Not-so-good-looking hippos and rhinos;
Sea-lions barking as they wait to be fed;
Chattering monkeys and dozing crocodiles;
Elephants and camels to ride upon;
. . . and so many, many others.
Thank you, God, for making all these fine animals;
Thank you for places where we can see them;
And thank you for those who look after them.

For other prayers see COUNTRY p. 47, SEA AND SHORE pp. 48–9, SCHOOL JOURNEYS AND VISITS p. 142

For all the strength we have,
To run and leap and play,
For all our limbs so sound and strong,
We thank thee, Lord, today.

For all the power we have
To feel and hear and see,
For all thy beauty round about,
Our praises rise to thee.[23]

Thank you, dear God, for so many different toys and games to enjoy......................... And thank you for other children to play with. Help us to play happily together without squabbling so that we can all have fun.

Dear Father God, there are lots of games we like playing in the playground. Thank you for the fun we can have with our friends. Please help us to be fair and happy when we play .... and help us, too, not to interfere with other children's games.

Thank you, dear God, for games to play
And other children to play with.
It is nice to win, to be first,
To be 'king of the castle'.
But we cannot always win:
Someone has to lose – life is like that!
So please help us to be good losers.

Dear Father God, we have so many different kinds of game to play, some with others and some by ourselves. We just want to say thank you for so much to enjoy.

Ask children what kind of things they collect.
Dear God, most of us enjoy collecting things . . . like stamps
. . . picture cards . . . badges . . . postcards . . . seashells . . .
Please show us how to get the most enjoyment from our
collecting by taking care with our collections; and help us to
learn lots of things through what we are doing.

Dear God, there are some times when we like to do our own
thing – to get out our paint boxes and paint a picture, to make a
scarf for a favourite doll, to build a model aeroplane, or to play
with a model railway. Thank you, God, for hobbies and
pastimes that we can enjoy when we are on our own and
especially those which enable us to use our skill to make
something. Thank you for those who have taught us how to do
these things and thank you for giving us the skill and patience
to be able to do them.

Thank you, God, for our adventure playground with tree
walks, ropes, ladders and lots of things to climb on. We can
have lots of fun there. Please help us to be careful.

Dear God, thank you for our swimming pool. We enjoy our
swimming . . . and jumping into the water . . . and diving . . .
and splashing our friends. And thank you, too, for those who
are there to keep an eye on us or to teach us how to swim or
dive.

Dear God, we do enjoy our football. It's great! We like making
up our own teams in the playground or after school. We like
playing on our class games afternoon or in the school team. We
like watching it too, especially when........................ are playing.
Help us to enjoy our games of football by playing well and
fairly ourselves or by being good spectators at a match.

Safety

Dear God, when we are in the street, please help us to keep our eyes and ears open, to watch for traffic and never to play or run into the roadway without looking.

Dear God, when we are near anything that can be dangerous, please make us extra careful so that we come to no harm.

Thank you, dear God, for people who come into school to talk about road safety. Help us to remember all they say so that we may be safe from harm and danger.

Today, dear God, we are thinking of........................ who has had an accident in the street (and is in hospital). Please give *him* courage if *he* is in pain and make *him* well so that *he* can soon be back with us again.

(For *ACCIDENTS see also pages 166–7*)

Dear God, lots of people enjoy throwing things and sometimes it is all right to do so but so often accidents are caused and people are hurt when things are thrown in the wrong place or at the wrong time. Please help us to be careful and never to throw stones or other objects at other people or into places where they might be.

Help us always to remember, dear God, that it is dangerous to play with fire. Help us never to get too close to fires or play with fire in such a way that may cause us to be burned. Help us, too, never to play with matches or anything else that may cause a fire that could do a lot of damage.

Dear God, it is fun to climb,
To be high above the ground
On a ladder or up a tree;
But these may break
And we can have a nasty fall,
So please help us to take care of ourselves
By keeping our feet on the ground.

Dear God, we enjoy the sea but we know that it can be dangerous. The waves are much stronger than we are and the currents can carry us out to sea. So when we enjoy our days at the seaside, please help us to be extra careful.

Teach us, dear God, to be careful whenever we are near the water so that we do not slip in or get out of our depth, even though we may be able to swim.

Dear Father God, please help us to be careful at home, especially with things that can be harmful to us:
Saucepans and kettles of boiling water,
Electrical points and fittings,
Steps and staircases,
Windows and glass,
Sharp tools and metals,
Bottles of liquid,
Jars and bottles of pills and medicines.
We know how easy it is to have accidents with these.
Please help us to take care.

Dear God, you have given us life and health and strength. You have also given us active minds. Teach us to use our minds to think what *could* cause us harm and then avoid such things.

THANK YOU, GOD, FOR LITTLE THINGS

Things I like best
are little things,
Like baby birds
and fluffy chicks,
the puppies down the street;
a shiny rock,
My little jeep,
The buttercups we pick;
A baby calf,
Some kittens,
Our playhouse just so big.
Jesus, You were little once,
You know how it is. [12]

Catherine Marshall

For sausages, baked beans and crisps
For papers full of fish and chips
For ice cream full of chocolate bits
Thanks, God.
For furry caterpillars to keep
For woodlice with their tickly feet
For crabs we catch with bits of meat
Thanks, God.
For bicycles and roller skates
For playing football with my mates
For times when I can stay up late
Thanks, God. [14]

Thank you, God, for water.
It may not seem very interesting
But we cannot live without it.
So thank you, God, for fresh water
And for those who made it fit to drink.

Dear Father God, there are lots of everyday things that we do not think much about –
Things like radio, television and video,
Refrigerators, freezers and washing machines,
Telephones, sewing machines and tape recorders,
Cookers, computers and central heating.
All these, and many other household gadgets, even electric lights, were unknown not so long ago. So thank you, God, for so much that is useful, and thank you for those who invented all these things.

Do you know, God, there are lots of things in our world that we never really notice? They are ordinary, everyday things that we take for granted because they are always there – things like trees, buses, salt, clothes and chairs. That is a strange list, and there are lots of others we could mention. So perhaps we can just say, 'Thank you, God, for everyday things.'

Dear God, help us to remember that some of the greatest riches of this world are things that money cannot buy:
The beauty of a tiny flower;
The glory of the sunset;
The warmth of summer sunshine;
A glass of cold water on a hot day;
The companionship of a pet;
The love of other people.
Help us to treasure such things and remember that there are so many others that have been given by you.

O God our Father, we would thank thee for all the bright things of life. Help us to see them, and to count them, and to remember them, that our lives may flow in ceaseless praise; for the sake of Jesus Christ our Lord.[12]

Rev. J. H. Jowett

Dear God, we say thank you for our books:
  For people who wrote them;
  For those who drew the pictures;
  For people who made them;
  And those who bought them
  So that we could enjoy them.
    Thank you God.

Praise to God for tiny things,
Shining stones, shimmering wings,
Peas in pods, so neatly pressed,
Exploring ants, never at rest.
If all these are in Your care,
We can trust You anywhere.

Praise to God for things of might,
Forest's depth and mountain's height,
Thunder's bolt and lightning's flash,
Hidden power in water's splash.
If all these are in Your care,
We can trust You anywhere.[22]

Before the prayer, ask children to name their favourite foods
Dear Father God, thank you for the food we enjoy:
  Fish and chips
  Bangers and beans   (*Add or substitute*
  Fruit jelly and ice-cream   *children's favourites*)
  Cream cakes
  Chocolate biscuits
  ....

Thank you that we have so many lovely things to eat. Help us
to remember those children in many places who have none of
these foods.

Dear God, we have lots of toys to enjoy. Some we have had for a long time and others are new ones. We have grown very fond of some and take them to bed with us. Thank you for our toys and for those who gave them to us.

Invite children to say how they like to enjoy themselves.
Dear God, we are all different and we enjoy ourselves in lots of different ways.
    Some of us like playing football;
    Others like painting or drawing.
    Some of us like playing music;
    And others like listening to it.
    Most of us enjoy reading books or comics:
    We also enjoy........................ (*children's suggestions*)
Thank you for giving us so much to enjoy and for the happiness these things give us.

Dear God, we do enjoy going into the sweet shop with a little money to spend on what we choose from all the bars of chocolate, sweets in jars, packets and boxes – and we enjoy eating what we have bought. But, please God, don't let us be greedy: help us to share our enjoyment with others.

Include in the following prayer anything which the children have grown themselves.
Thank you, God, for things we can grow:
    Mustard and cress
    Beans in jars
    Bulbs in bowls
    Flowers in the garden
    ....
Thank you for the fun of growing them. Help us to remember that, although we look after them, it is you, not us, that make them grow.

A PRAYER FOUND IN CHESTER CATHEDRAL

Give me a good digestion, Lord,
    And also something to digest;
Give me a healthy body, Lord,
    With sense to keep it at its best,
Give me a healthy mind, good Lord,
    To keep the good and pure in sight,
Which seeing sin is not appalled
    But finds a way to set it right;
Give me a mind that is not bored,
    That does not whimper, whine or sigh;
Don't let me worry overmuch
    About the fussy thing called I.
Give me a sense of humour, Lord,
    Give me the grace to see a joke,
To get some happiness from life
    And pass it on to other folk.

Anonymous

ATTITUDES AND FEELINGS

Thanks be to thee, our Lord Jesus Christ,
For all the benefits thou hast won for us,
For all the pains and insults thou hast borne for us.
O most merciful Redeemer, Friend and Brother,
May we see thee more clearly,
Love thee more dearly
And follow thee more nearly
Day by day,
For thine own dear sake.

St. Richard of Chichester

Dear God . . .
    Teach us to love;
    Teach us to care;
    Teach us to comfort;
    Teach us to share.
    Teach us true kindness,
    Goodness and grace,
    Joy in each heart,
    And smiles on each face.

Dear God, it isn't fair. There are some people who have a lot more things than we have. But that's life! We know that there are lots of things that may not seem fair and so we ask that you will help us to be content with and thankful for all we have.

Dear Father God, so often we think the worst of other people and then find out we were wrong. Please help us not to make hasty decisions.

Dear God, it is so easy to find fault with others when we do or say the same kind of thing ourselves. Please forgive us if we do and help us to try to put ourselves right.

Dear Father God, I hope I am not the kind of person that others can't stand. If I am, please help me to change.

Dear God, as black notes and white notes on a piano can together make harmony, may black and white folk work together to bring harmony to the world.

Thank you, Father God, for making everybody different. Thank you for making me just like I am – not like any of those who are around me. But help me to remember that does not make me *better* than they are, nor let me think that I am always right. You have made us all and we are all your children.

Dear God, if we think we are always right, forgive us for thinking too much of ourselves and help us to learn that other people sometimes know better than we do.

Dear God, there are some things which so easily spoil our relationships with others:
Being bad tempered or sulky;
Always wanting our own way;
Taking things which do not belong to us;
Cheating and being untruthful;
.... (*add others*).
Please help us to avoid such things.

Thank you, God, for colours:
For colours of flowers that welcome the spring;
For the many-coloured beauties of the summer garden;
For leaves of many colours making autumn so beautiful;
For wintry scenes of black and white and brown.
Thank you, God, for showing us that many colours can make beautiful scenes. Help us to see how people of different colours can work together to make a beautiful world.

A Prayer of the Sioux Indians
O Great Spirit, help me never to judge another until I have walked two weeks in his moccasins.[12]

Friendship and loyalty

Dear God, please help me to be gentle, kind and unselfish, a friend to those in need and one upon whom others can rely.

Thank you, dear God, for our friends but help us to know how important it is for us to make friends with those children who have no friends and would greatly value our friendship.

'A friend in need is a friend indeed.'
Dear God, please make me such a friend.

Dear God, it is not nice when someone we called a friend is unkind to us, turns against us or lets us down. Please help us always to be loyal to our friends so that they do not feel let down by us.

Dear God,
Teach me the way of friendship
So that I can be a good friend
To someone who needs me –
Someone who feels left out
Or is lonely . . .
Just as Jesus befriended Matthew
And Zacchaeus, whom no one liked.
Help me to be like Jesus –
A friend to anyone who needs me.

Lord Jesus, You were friendly with the people whom no one liked. Please make us friendly with them, too.[28]

Zinnia Bryan

Dear God,
There are times when I like to do things with others,
To be part of a team or gang,
So that we can do things together.
Teach me how to be a good member of the team,
Working or playing unselfishly,
And being friendly and loyal to my team mates.

Teach me, O God, the meaning of friendship:
    To like people for what they are
    And not for what they might give me;
    To share whatever I have
    Even though my friends have little to share with me;
    To do things my friends would like to do
    Even though I may want to do something else;
    To be loyal to my friends
    Even if that makes me unpopular with others.
Above all, teach me how to give of myself, for that is the very
best I can offer to my friends.

        Dear God, please make me loyal . . .
        Loyal to my family;
        Loyal to my friends;
        Loyal to my school;
        Loyal to my country;
        Loyal to my beliefs;
        Loyal to you.
        And, if it is difficult
        To do any of these,
        Please give me extra strength.

Dear God, we want to serve you as best we can. Help us to
think more of you than we do of ourselves and to be loyal to
those things in which we believe.

Love and unselfishness

Dear God, thank you for the love of our parents: help us to show our love for them. Thank you for the love of our friends: help us to love them too. Thank you, God, for your great love: help us to love you and all your children everywhere.

Dear Father God, we remember how Jesus told his friends to love one another. Help us to do this ourselves.

Dear God, grant that when we think too much of ourselves we may have that love in our hearts which makes us think even more of others.

Dear God,
You have shown us what love really is;
You loved us so much that you sent us your Son, Jesus;
And because you loved us, we want to love you.
Yet we cannot see you
And our words alone may not seem very much,
So help us to show our love for you
By loving and helping others who need our love
For we know this is what you would wish us to do.

Lord God, love is something special:
  the more we receive,
    the more we want to give away;
  the more we try to keep it for ourselves,
    the less we have to give.
It is like a puzzle that is hard to solve,
  a riddle that has no answer.
But we know it is true, that love works this way.
We give love to others, and others give it back:
  love is shared, and sharing it is lovely.[22]

Dear God,
I'm sorry, but there are some people I just don't like!

I know that you love everybody, even the bad people and the people who don't love you, but I can't manage it.

Please help me to remember how much you love everyone; help me not to be nasty in return if someone is nasty to me.

I've just remembered – there were people who didn't like Jesus too. So he knows what it is like.

Help me to be kind to people.[28]

David Lewis

O God, who hast prepared for them that love thee such good things as pass man's understanding: pour into our hearts such love toward thee, that we, loving thee above all things, may obtain thy promises, which exceed all that we can desire; through Jesus Christ our Lord.[1]

Book of Common Prayer

Lord, I know that one of the best ways I can show my love for you is by serving other people

Sometimes this is easy – when I am with people I like.
Please help me when loving is hard,
    When people are unkind,
    When they don't understand,
    When I just don't like them.
Teach me to love as you loved
    when you were walking about in Palestine.
Teach me to love as you love now –
    everyone . . . always.[14]

Brother Kenneth and Sister Geraldine

Dear God, some of the children I know are so selfish: they want everything for themselves. Please help me not to be like that but help me to be ready to share or lend or give to others – even the selfish ones.

Courage and perseverance

Heavenly Father, give us courage to say 'no' when other people try to persuade us to do what we know to be wrong.[16]

Beryl Bye

Dear Father God, there are some things which happen which make us afraid. There are some people who scare us, too. When we are afraid, please make us brave and give us courage, knowing that you, our Father, are never far away.

O God, give me the courage to face up to the difficulties of life . . . but also the sense not to put myself in harm's way by doing anything reckless or foolish.

Forgive us, dear God, for those times when we take the easy way out instead of standing up for what we know to be right. Give us courage always to be true to our beliefs and to you.

Father, hear the prayer we offer;
Not for ease that prayer shall be,
But for strength that we may ever
Live our lives courageously.

Mrs. Love Maria Willis

Dear God, give us courage:
    Courage to go on when in difficulty;
    Courage to face all our problems with cheerfulness;
    Courage to stand up for what is right;
    Courage to be true to our beliefs.
At all times when we need that extra courage, dear God grant us your help.

Dear Father God, when my work seems difficult and I can't seem to get it right, please help me to keep on trying and not give in too easily.

Dear God, if anything does not seem to go right with our work today, please help us not to take the easy way out and give in, but help us to put our minds to what we are doing until we find the right way to do the work.

Lord Jesus, who never gave in in face of difficulties, danger and even death, help us to follow your example and persevere in all that we have to do.

Teach us, O God, to do what needs to be done when it needs to be done and not to put off until tomorrow what we ought to be doing today.

O God, give us 'stickability'.
Help us not to give in when something is difficult,
Or neglect our duties to do what pleases us,
But to keep at our appointed task until it is finished.

Dear God, sometimes we feel like giving up:
Sometimes our work seems difficult;
Sometimes we can't understand our work;
Sometimes we don't seem to have time;
Sometimes just about everything seems to go wrong.
At times such as these, please God help us to keep our minds on what we are doing, to try our hardest, and to persevere until we have completed what we are doing.

Service

Dear Father God, you have given us so much. Help us to show our thanks by using our gifts to help others, especially any in need.

Dear God, before I come to the end of today, please help me to have done at least one thing to help somebody else.

> Help us, dear God:
> To be more ready to give than to receive;
> To be more willing to help other people;
> To be more thoughtful for the needs of others;
> To be more ready to share those things we have;
> And, in doing so, to find for ourselves
> The true happiness that money can never buy.

Dear God, when we think of all that you have given us, we know that we can never fully thank you. But we do know that you need us to serve you and that we can best do so by serving others in your Name. Please show us the best way to do so.

Lord Jesus, in days of old you called people with the words 'Follow Me' and some of them did. Help us to listen to your words and follow your instructions.

Lord Jesus, please make us like the good Samaritan, always ready to stop and help when we come across someone in trouble. Make us ready to help even when we are busy or when it is someone we don't like very much or do not know.
    We ask it because we want to be like you.[28]

Zinnia Bryan

A Muslim prayer from the great prayer book of Islam
O Allah (God)! make me one of those persons who rejoice in
the doing of good deeds and fervently pray for Thy forgiveness
if they happen to go wrong.

> Teach us, good Lord
> To serve thee as thou deservest,
> To give and not to count the cost,
> To fight and not to heed the wounds,
> To toil and not to seek for rest,
> To labour and not to ask for any reward,
> Save that of knowing that we do thy will.
>
> *St. Ignatius Loyola*

Dear God, teach us that in serving others in your Name we are
serving you. May we do so gladly and find joy in our service.

Dear God, show us some means of serving others and helping
them along life's way:
    By giving a cheery word or a happy smile;
    By offering a helping hand, or feet to run their errands;
    By using some of our time and energy to help them;
    By making a gift of something that means much to us.
And help us to discover for ourselves that the more we give to
others the greater will be our blessing.

Dear God,
Sometimes we have so much to do that we wonder how we can
find time to do all that needs to be done. But you have given us
twenty-four hours every day. Help us to use our time wisely so
that each day there is time to do something for other people
and time to spend with you.

Sorry!

Loving heavenly Father, we are glad that we belong to Your big family. Help us to live as Your happy children. Sometimes we do unkind and foolish things that make You sad. Help us to say 'I'm sorry'; and show us how we can become more helpful, kind, and loving every day.[4]

Lord Jesus, we remember how you forgave the people who hurt you. Help us to forgive those who hurt us. May we never try to pay them back.[12]

Brenda Holloway

Dear God, sometimes I hurt other people by the things
I say or do and sometimes I am selfish or lose my temper.
I am sorry for these things. Please help me to do better.

Dear God, we don't want to do anything today that is wrong or hurtful, but if we do, please help us to admit our faults and say we are sorry.

Dear God, saying 'sorry' is not easy but if I hurt anyone today, please help me to say that I am sorry, just as I would like them to do if they do anything that may hurt or upset me.

Dear God,
It isn't easy to forgive,
Especially when someone has hurt us;
But you will forgive our wrong doings
And we ask you to help us to forgive others . . .
And then try to forget.

Father God, sometimes our friends hurt us. When this happens help us not to hit back. Help us to forgive them as Jesus taught us to do, and help us to make friends again quickly.[22]

Lord Jesus Christ, we have sometimes been rude to our parents and teachers. We have answered back when we have been told off. We have been impolite and cheeky to people we have met. We are sorry. Please forgive us, for you died to take away our sins.[28]

Zinnia Bryan

For foolish things I do each day
And all the hurtful things I say,
Upsetting those who call me friend
And driving others 'round the bend';
    Dear God, I'm sorry!

A Hindu prayer for forgiveness from the Vedas
Whatever sins have been committed by me, by thought, word or deed, may the supreme Lord, the source of strength, wisdom and purity, forgive me and cleanse me of them all.

Dear God, we ask forgiveness for all we have done wrong:
    For all our unkind words that have hurt others,
        Forgive us, God our Father;
    For things we have done that we know to be wrong,
        Forgive us, God our Father;
    For sometimes losing control of ourselves,
        Forgive us, God our Father;
    For thinking more of ourselves than we do of you,
        Forgive us, God our Father.
Forgive us, dear God, and help us to do better.

Happiness and sadness

This prayer could be accompanied by actions.

When we are happy, Father God,
    we like to sing,
    we like to laugh,
    we like to jump about,
    we like to dance,
    we like to clap our hands.
It is good for us to be happy.
Thank you, God, for happiness.
Show us how we can help to make others happy, too.[22]

O God, we thank thee for making us happy
at home and at school.
Help us to make other people happy too,
For Jesus Christ's sake.[4]

Because we are so happy,
help us to make someone else happy,
For Jesus Christ's sake.[4]

Dear God, there are times when we feel so happy that we just want to sing or dance and tell others of our joy. Thank you for making us happy. Please help us to share our happiness with others.

Sometimes happy, sometimes sad,
Sometimes gloomy, sometimes glad:
Joys and sorrows come and go
Thank you, Father, that you know
And that you love and that you care:
For all our needs, Lord, hear our prayer.

Dear God, please give me a smiling face and a happy way with me so that, no matter how I feel myself, I am still able to make other people happier.

Dear Lord, remind us that –
  Happiness comes from loving,
  Happiness comes from giving,
  Happiness comes from caring,
  Happiness comes from sharing,
  Happiness comes from working,
  Happiness comes from worshipping the One who has shown the world the only way of true happiness.[16]

Beryl Bye

Sometimes, dear God, we feel so sad that we have a good cry. Help us never to be ashamed of our tears and help us to know that we can always share our sadness with you, knowing that you care and can comfort.

Dear God, we get so upset about things sometimes that we feel very unhappy.
  Other children say things that are not very nice;
  Sometimes they do things which are hurtful;
  Some of them are spiteful or bad tempered;
  Some will not let us join in their games;
  Some get very sulky if they do not have their own way.
Please help us not to get upset about things, but even more important, please teach us to make sure that we do not do the same things ourselves.

If I am feeling sad, O Lord,
Please help me not to be a misery
Upsetting others as well as myself.

Attitudes and feelings

There are times, dear God, when we get so angry that we lose our tempers or say and do things that are hurtful to others. Please help us all through today to control our tempers, to guard our tongues and keep our hands to ourselves.

Dear God, forgive us if we are jealous of other people or covet their belongings. Help us to make the most of what we have and to be content.

Take from us, O God, any form of pride in ourselves and any boasting of our achievements. Teach us the ways of true humility.

Dear God, there are some people who always want more than they have, or more than their fair share of anything that is going. Please guard us from the sin of being greedy.

Dear God, sometimes when someone has hurt us very much, we say, 'I can never forgive him for that.' Please help us if we think like that for, if we do not forgive others, we cannot expect you to forgive us for the things we do wrong. Help us, dear God, to forgive.

Dear God, we all have money to use. We know how important it is for buying the things we need. It makes some people very happy and it makes some people unhappy because they always want more than they have. Please teach us to use our money wisely, to know the pleasure of buying things, the importance of saving and the happiness we get when we give some away to someone who has less than we have.

O God, help us not to despise or oppose what we do not understand.

William Penn

Dear God, there are times when we are very disappointed:
    When someone fails to keep a promise;
    When we are unable to go on a special visit;
    When somebody picks up the book that *we* wanted;
    When someone else is chosen for a job *we* wanted;
    When........................ (*refer to any particular circumstance*).
Help us to bear our disappointment bravely and to remember that perhaps we shall not be disappointed 'next time'.

Forgive us, O Lord, that so often we are selfish.
    We want the best always for ourselves.
    We want to have everything our way.
    We keep things that we ought to share with others.
    We have little thought for the feelings of others
    But we expect them to do things for us.
Grant unto us, O Lord, a right attitude to others and help us to think more of them than we do of ourselves.

Dear God, how easy it is to be selfish and keep things to ourselves. Teach us how to share what we have and to do so without letting everybody else know.

Dear God, there are some things we don't like having to do but people expect us to do them. Help us to remember that we cannot do as we want all the time but we have to share the tasks as well as the enjoyable things in life. So help us today happily to acept all that needs to be done.

Fears and worries

Dear Father God, sometimes I worry about things. When I do, please help me to know that you are always near and ready to help me.

Dear God, whenever we are afraid, please help us to remember that you are always near and we have no need to fear.

> Dear God, we know that you love us
> And we trust you to care for us
> So please help us to remember
> That we have nothing to fear.

Most loving Lord, give me a childlike love of Thee, which may cast out all fear.

E. B. Pusey

> When worries come and fears invade,
> We come to you and ask for aid;
> Lord, make us calm and unafraid.

Dear God, forgive us that we so often let you down.
We want to do what is right but sometimes we are afraid.
We are afraid of what others may say;
We are afraid of what others may do;
We are afraid that they may laugh at us;
We are afraid of becoming unpopular.
Forgive us, dear God,
And help us to follow the example of Jesus,
Who feared no one
But remained true to you to the end of his life on earth.

We trust you, Lord to guide us
Through worry, doubt and fear;
For knowing you're beside us
Helps problems disappear.

Dear God, we worry about so many things which never happen but we do not seem to learn and we keep on worrying. Please help us not to worry about tomorrow or what may happen but to place our trust in you and live our lives to the full.

Dear God, you must sometimes think we are rather strange people.
    We worry about things that may never happen.
    We worry because we cannot do things, when all we need do is ask for help.
    We worry about what tomorrow may bring.
We remember how Jesus told people not to worry because you care for those who trust in you. Next time we start worrying, please help us to remember this and look to you for help.

Dear God, sometimes we get worried or upset when things do not seem to go right. Teach us not to worry but to trust that you will guide and strengthen us through all our difficulties.

Dear God,
Please help us to overcome temptations
And give us peace in our minds:
Free us from anxieties and fears
And from all unnecessary worries:
Teach us to trust in you for all things,
Knowing that you are our Father.

A Hindu morning prayer from the Vedas
        O Lord, hear my call:
        I cry to you longing for help;
        Be good to me this day.
        O wise God, you are Lord of all,
        You are King of heaven and earth;
        Hear my prayer.

Three Jewish prayers from the book of Psalms in the Bible
        Create a pure heart in me, O God
        and put a new and loyal spirit in me.[3]

Psalm 51; 10

Teach me, Lord, what you want me to do,
    and I will obey you faithfully;
    teach me to serve you with complete devotion.
I will praise you with all my heart,
    O Lord my God;
I will proclaim your greatness for ever.[3]

Psalm 86; 11–12

Examine me, O God, and know my mind;
    test me, and discover my thoughts.
Find out if there is any evil in me
    and guide me in the everlasting way.[3]

Psalm 139; 23–24

Father, lead me day by day
Ever in Thine own sweet way;
Teach me to be pure and true,
Show me what I ought to do.

John Page Hopps

O Lord, open my eyes, to see what is beautiful:
My mind, to know what is true,
My heart, to love what is good:
For Jesus' sake.[24]

Today, O God, make me
  Brave enough to face the things of which I am afraid;
  Strong enough to overcome the temptations which try to
    make me do the wrong thing and not to do the right thing;
  Persevering enough to finish every task that is given me to
    do;
  Kind enough always to be ready to help others;
  Obedient enough to obey your voice whenever you speak to
    me through my conscience.
Help me
  To live in purity;
  To speak in truth;
  To act in love
    All through today.
This I ask for Jesus' sake.[7]

Dr. William Barclay

    Sometimes I'm not sure what to do,
    Or where to go, or what to say –
    To do what's good and right and true;
    In need of one to show the way.
    Dear God, please be my guide today.

From the Buddhist scriptures
Teach us, O Blessed One, control of speech, control of thought,
control of action. Help us to keep these roads of action clear
and so find the Way made known by Thee to the wise in
heart.[11]

Lord, make me an instrument of thy
peace. Where there is hatred, let me
sow love. Where there is injury,
pardon. Where there is doubt, faith.
Where there is despair, hope. Where
there is darkness, light. Where there
is sadness, joy.

O Divine Master, grant that I may
not so much seek to be consoled as to
console; to be understood, as to
understand; to be loved, as to love;
for it is in giving that we receive,
it is in pardoning that we are pardoned,
and it is in dying that we are born to
Eternal Life.

St. Francis of Assisi

OUR NATION AND OTHERS

God bless our native land!
May heaven's protecting hand
   Still guard our shore:
May peace her power extend,
Foe be transformed to friend
And Britain's rights depend
   On war no more.

Nor on this land alone,
But be God's mercies known
   From shore to shore:
Lord make the nations see
That men should brothers be,
And form one family
   The wide world o'er.

William Edward Hickson

Queen and country

Dear God, bless our Queen and her family and help them in all they do.

We say thank you, dear God, for our Queen and the members of the royal family, who give pleasure to so many people. Please bless them in all they do and give them good health so that they may continue to do so for many years.

Dear God, bless our Queen.
Help her to reign over us wisely and well.
Help her to serve Britain and all its people.
Help her in all the duties she has to perform.
Help her when she represents our nation.
Help her to set an example that all may follow.
And help all those who advise or support her.

THE NATIONAL ANTHEM
God save our gracious Queen;
Long live our noble Queen;
　God save the Queen!
Send her victorious,
Happy and glorious,
Long to reign over us.
　God save the Queen!

Thy choicest gifts in store
On her be pleased to pour;
　Long may she reign;
May she defend our laws,
And ever give us cause
To sing with heart and voice:
　'God save the Queen!'

Attrib. to Henry Carey

Dear God, we think of our royal family, the Queen, the Duke of Edinburgh, the Prince and Princess of Wales and all the others. They go to many places to do many different things and people are very pleased to see them. People expect, too, that they will always set a good example. So, please help them, God, to do their duties well and help us to be loyal to them.

Dear God,
We love the pageantry and colour of state occasions, the coaches with their fine horses, the military bands and colourful uniforms, the marching and the music. We enjoy seeing the royal family and other important people, perhaps in person or when watching the event on television. We like to see so many other people enjoying themselves too.
[Tomorrow we have a holiday from school because .... We ask that it may be an enjoyable time for everybody and that nothing will spoil the pleasure.]
Thank you, God, for our Queen and her family and for all others who give us such pleasure.

O God, bless our land and all its people:
Help us all to work together to make it a land
of freedom, justice, understanding and peace.

Dear God,
Thank you for all the blessings of living in this land;
For all that has been handed down to us from the past
And for the freedom that is ours today.
Give wisdom to all our leaders,
A sense of responsibility to all our people
And, to us, a desire to grow up to be good citizens,
Ready to pass on to others
Even more than was passed down to us.

Government and leaders

Dear God, we ask you to bless our Prime Minister and all members of the Government. Please help them in all they have to do for the good of our country and its people.

> Dear God,
> Please guide our Prime Minister,
> And all Members of Parliament.
> Help them to govern us well
> And make good laws:
> Help us to keep the laws
> And grow up to be good citizens.

Hear our prayer, O God, for all who have responsibility for the governing of our land – the Queen and her ministers, the elected Members of Parliament and the Lords. May your Spirit be their guide in all their duties and responsibilities toward our nation and the world. Grant that they may make wise decisions and good laws which are in the interests of our people as a whole so that the nation may prosper and its people live at peace with their neighbours.

Dear God, we remember before you all who are called to rule our nation and those who are appointed to positions of power and authority. Grant unto them wisdom and self-control, discipline and patience, wise judgement and a sense of responsibility. So may we be free from fear, injustice and all that would prevent us from living full and happy lives.

Dear God, we ask your guidance for all who have positions of authority in our land – the Queen and her Ministers, all the elected Members of Parliament and those who advise them – so that they may govern our nation wisely and well.

A Fourteenth Century prayer from the Service of the Knights of the Garter
O God, Almighty Father, King of Kings and Lord of all our rulers, grant that the minds of all who go out as leaders before us, the statesmen, the judges, the men of learning and the men of wealth, may be so filled with the love of thy laws, and of that which is righteous and life-giving, that they may serve as a wholesome salt unto the earth, and be worthy servants of thy good and perfect gifts; through Jesus Christ our Lord.

Dear God, hear our prayers for those people who hold important positions as heads of government departments or leaders in the world of business and industry.
   May those who advise government ministers give sound advice that is in the interest of the people of our land.
   May those in business, whose decisions may affect not only their business but the jobs of many who work in it, be given good judgement enabling them to decide wisely.

We remember, dear God, those who have responsibility for representing workers in the Trade Union movement – the General Secretary and members of the Trade Union Congress, the secretaries, officers and committees of the various unions. Give them wisdom to make decisions that are not only in the interests of their members but also of the needs of all people in our country.

Hear our prayer, dear God, for the leaders of the churches in our land; Archbishops and Bishops, Presidents and others who hold high office in the various Christian denominations. Bless, too, those who meet in synods, conferences, councils and other meetings to make important decisions. Guide them by your Holy Spirit so that your Church may grow and bear its witness faithfully to the people of this land.

Local government

We thank you, dear God, for those people who are responsible for our *city/town/neighbourhood*:
> The Mayor (Chairman/Provost);
> The Councillors;
> Members of Committees.

Help them to make good decisions that are for the good of all the people who live here.

Dear God, our Mayor and Councillors are very busy people who have to spend a lot of time in meetings. Please give them any help and strength they need.

We think today, dear God, of all the people who have been elected to the Council and have to decide how the money should be spent so that people who live here can have the best possible education, housing, libraries, sports, parks and lots of other things. Please help them to do what will be best for the people of our *town*.

Dear God, there are lots of people who work in our *town/district* and do things for us. Thank you for those in charge of departments and all who work in the offices; for people in schools, social workers, librarians and park keepers; for road menders, road sweepers, refuse collectors and all who help look after our *town*.

Thank you, dear God, for the parks, playing fields and play-grounds where we can play with our friends or in matches against other schools, or where we can enjoy a picnic or the beautiful flowers. Thank you, too, for the people on the council who make plans for our open spaces and for the park keepers and groundsmen who look after them.

An election

Today (*tomorrow*), dear God, lots of people will be voting to decide who will serve in the Government (*on the Council*). Please help them to vote wisely.

Dear God, *tomorrow* is voting day, when people in all parts of this land will be electing men and women to serve as Members of Parliament. Please help all people to vote wisely, to elect whoever *they* believe to be the right person and not to be wrongly persuaded by what others have to say. And grant, dear God, that those who are elected may be the men and women who will best be able to serve our country in Parliament.

After an election
Dear God, yesterday we had an election and now we have a change of government.

We pray for our Prime Minister and ask that *he* may be guided by you when choosing the new ministers of the government.

We pray for all who will have special responsibilities, that they may be given wisdom when carrying out their duties.

We pray for all who have been elected, that they may faithfully attend to their parliamentary duties and honestly represent those who elected them.

We pray for our new government that it may pass only those laws which are for the good of our land.

We pray for all our people, that, whether they are pleased or disappointed with the result, they may accept the members of our fairly elected government as their representatives.

Lord, please bless our land and all our people.

We think, today, dear God, of all those people who have been elected as Members of Parliament. Sometimes it is very difficult for them to know what is the right decision to make. So please, help them to make wise decisions that will be for the good of our land and its people.

Times of trouble or unrest

Dear God, in this time of trouble, we ask that you will look down upon our land and grant us your protection from all that would take from us the freedom and justice that we have long enjoyed. Then grant, we pray, that we may live in peace with our neighbours and enjoy the fruits of our work.

O God, our help in ages past,
Our hope for years to come,
Be Thou our guard while troubles last
And our eternal home.

Isaac Watts

Dear God, be with all the men, women and children who are in danger or afraid because of the fighting in........................ and give them your strength. May the fighting soon end.

Dear God, we are sorry that some of our soldiers, sailors and airmen are having to fight in........................ Be with them and protect them as they do their duties: strengthen their families who wait anxiously at home; and grant that the fighting may soon be brought to an end.

Almighty Father, who dost give
The gift of life to all who live,
Look down upon earth's sin and strife,
And lift us to a nobler life.

Lift up our hearts, O King of Kings,
To brighter hopes and kindlier things,
To visions of a larger good,
And holier dreams of brotherhood.

John Masterman

Listen, Lord, to my prayer; hear my cries for help. I call to you in times of trouble because you answer my prayers.[3]

Psalm 86; vv. 6–7

Dear God, the....................... *workers* are going on strike and this will cause hardship for a lot of people. Please help everyone to sort out their differences so that it may soon end.

Before a protest march or demonstration
Dear God, we thank you that in our country people are free to say what they like and to protest at things they think are wrong. Tomorrow lots of people are going to protest about........................ May they do so peacefully and without any unpleasantness so that no one is hurt.

On an outbreak of war, fighting or invasion
Dear God, we are sorry to hear about the *fighting* in .... May it soon come to an end and the leaders meet to find a way to bring peace to that troubled land. In the meantime we ask that you will be with all who lose loved ones or homes and all who suffer injury or hardship. Please help all the nations of the world to learn·the ways of peace.

A prayer after an act of terrorism
O God, we were very sad to hear about the *bomb explosion* in........................ which killed and hurt many people. Give comfort to all who are in pain and those who mourn. We cannot understand why anyone would want to harm innocent people and we ask that others may realise that this is not the way to get support for what they want.

The prayers on page 167 could also be used.

International co-operation

A prayer for use on United Nations Day
Dear God, hear our prayer for all the peoples of the world that they may live in peace and enjoy the fruits of the earth. We remember especially those not as fortunate as we are, who have little to eat, who live in poverty or in lands torn by warfare. Grant your help to the United Nations Organisation and to all who seek to bring peace and prosperity to all peoples. May we, who have so much, show our gratitude by doing what we can to lift the burden for so many.

Prayers to use on Europe Day or Commonwealth Day
Almighty God, we say thank you for the Commonwealth [*or the community of nations*] of which our country is a member. Give us a spirit of understanding, co-operation and peace toward one another. Give to the leaders of the nations the inspiration of your Holy Spirit so that they may realise their responsibilities to work together for the good of each other and the glory of your Holy Name.

O God, our Father and Father of all the people on earth, hear our prayer as we remember peoples and nations in many parts of the world who form the Commonwealth. In our changing world, grant that each may have a spirit of understanding and peace toward the others. May the bonds of friendship formed in the past and their responsibilities toward the present age, enable all member countries to work together for the good of each other and the world in general.

We give thanks, O God, for the countries of Europe, for all the resources available, and for the skills of the people in industry and commerce. Thank you, too, that in recent years they have learned to work more closely together in many ways. Help our leaders that they may be able to remove such barriers as still divide us.

Prayers for international co-operation
Thank you, dear God, for the various ways in which the nations of the world have learned to work together. May they find other ways, too, so that, as they work together, people may discover that it is better to do so than to be suspicious of each other.

Dear God, where the nations in any part of the world join together to help or protect each other, grant that the power this gives them may never be used to take away the freedom or independence of others.

Dear God,
You have created a wonderful world,
Filled with power for man to use . . .
Coal, gas, electricity, oil . . .
And the tiny but mighty atom.
This is the nuclear age,
Giving boundless energy and power,
But also the power to destroy
With nuclear weapons.
Hear our prayer, dear God,
That those who have this power
May never use it,
But learn to live in peace
And so end the fears
Of people throughout the world.

A prayer for national harmony
Almighty God, we thank you for those lands where people of different races and beliefs have learned to live together in peace. We pray for all lands where there is fighting or mistrust and ask that those people may learn how to settle their differences and live peaceably together.

Freedom, order and justice

Dear God, thank you that we are free to do so many things that we like doing. As long as we keep the law we can say what we like, go where we like, do what we like and worship you in whatever way we like without having to fear what will happen. Hear our prayer for people in many parts of the world who do not have this freedom.

Dear Father God, thank you for all those people who help keep law and order in our country and see that justice is done.

Dear God, help us always to be law-abiding citizens of our land, doing only those things which we know to be right and helping all those whose duty it is to keep law and order.

Dear Father God, we know that you wish us to be good honest citizens and so we ask that you will make us willing and happy to keep all the laws of our land.

Dear God, we say thank you for our policemen and all who are responsible for keeping law and order in our land.
Thank you
 For the policemen and policewomen who patrol the streets;
 For those in cars and on motorcycles who move quickly;
 For mounted police and others who control crowds;
 For special squads and patrols for emergency work;
 For detectives and plain-clothes police.
We ask your help for all who have the responsibility for the running of our police forces that they may know the best way to do so; and we ask that people will be ready to help the police in their difficult task of seeing that the fair laws of our land are not broken and that those who do break them are brought to justice.

Dear God, wherever we go we find there are rules and laws that we are expected to keep.
We have to keep the rules when we play our games.
We have rules in our school and in class.
We have rules or laws to be kept by all the people who live in this country.
Help us to remember that these rules and laws are made for the good of everyone. Please help us to keep them.

Dear God, we know how difficult it is to decide what is right, especially when some people may not be telling the truth. We ask your help for all those who are responsible for justice in our country: for ordinary people who form juries that decide whether a person is guilty; for judges and magistrates who must pass sentence; for judges who must judge between people who cannot settle their differences. We ask that all may be wise, sound and fair in their judgements and that justice may be done.

Dear God, it must be very difficult to be a judge or a magistrate, listening to all the evidence and trying to decide what is the truth and what is not.
We know that you like to see justice done, and so we ask you to give them the wisdom, understanding and fairness that they need. Through Jesus Christ our Lord.[12]

Heavenly Father, we are so glad and thankful that we live in a land where people are free and the law is fair.
So we pray for those who rule our land, under Her Majesty the Queen: for the Prime Minister and the Cabinet; for all the Members of Parliament (especially the one who represents us); and for our Mayor and the local council.
Please give to all of them honesty and understanding, so that our country may be a place where you are honoured, and your laws obeyed. For Jesus Christ's sake.[12]

Peace and brotherhood

Dear God, we are all your children
And you are our Father.
That makes us all brothers and sisters
In a very special way.
So please help us to be *good* brothers and sisters
Who do not quarrel or hurt one another.

Dear Father God, there is so much trouble in the world with lots of people fighting and killing each other. Please teach people how to live in peace so that there will be no more wars and fighting.

Dear God, please give me peace in my heart, which will help me to make peace where I am, which will help to bring just a little more peace to the world.

Dear God, maker of all things,
The people of the world are all your children:
That makes us all brothers and sisters.
Please help us to love one another;
Teach the nations the ways of friendship and peace
And help us all to enjoy true peace and happiness.

A Muslim prayer
Praise be unto God, the Lord of Glory, and peace be upon his people.[11]

A Hindu prayer from the Upanishads
O God, the Peaceful, the Good, the One, bring us into thy Truth and Peace.[11]

A Brownie Guide's prayer for peace
O God, send thy Spirit into our hearts that we may hate war and love peace. Teach the children of every land that it is better to love one another than to fight, so that war and bitterness may cease, and thy kingdom of love may be set up through all the world; for the sake of Jesus Christ our Lord.[29]

A Jewish prayer from the Liberal Prayer Book
We pray for all mankind. Though divided into nations and races, yet we all are Thy children, drawing from Thee our life and being. Cause hatred and strife to vanish, that abiding peace may fill the earth, and all men may be blessed. So shall the spirit of brotherhood among men show forth their faith that Thou art the Father of all.[26]

A prayer of Bahá'u'lláh (Bahá'í)
O my God! Unite the hearts of Thy servants and reveal to them Thy Great Purpose. May they follow Thy Commandments and abide in Thy Law. Help them, O God, in their endeavour, and grant them strength to serve Thee. O God leave them not to themselves, but guide their steps by the light of Thy knowledge and cheer their hearts by Thy love, Verily, Thou art their Helper and their Lord.[2]

'Blessed are the peacemakers: for they shall be called the children of God.' Lord, help us to become such children of God.

Dear God, fill our hearts, and the hearts of all people, with your spirit of peace, so that we may live at peace with our neighbours in brotherhood and with love.

A prayer of a child in Northern Ireland:

Father God, some of us know
what it is to be afraid to talk to people
of a different religion.
We are afraid because of what our
parents will say or do to us.
We are afraid because of what our
neighbours will say or do to us.
Give us courage.
Teach children and grown-ups in this
and every land
to show love to people
no matter what colour they are
or by what name they are called.[15]

OUR SCHOOL

This is our school,
Let peace dwell here,
Let the room be full of contentment.
Let love abide here,
Love of one another,
Love of mankind,
Love of life itself,
And love of God.
Let us remember
That as many hands build a house,
So many hearts make a school.[35]

The School Creed of a Canadian school

Our school

This is *our* school, dear God, and we spend a lot of our time here. Please help us to enjoy it.

Dear Father God, help us to think of the people in our school as one big family – a happy family in which we all try to help each other.

Dear God, be with us today in our school and help us all to do what we can to make it a happy place.

> O Lord, bless our school:
> That, working together
>   and playing together,
> We may learn to serve thee,
>   and to serve one another:
> For Jesus' sake.[24]

Dear God,
Thank you for my classroom with all the lovely bright pictures hanging on the walls, and the tables where we work.
   Thank you for all the new things there are to learn every day – about space travel and music and how to make things.
   Please help me to try hard to do things, even when I find them difficult.[28]

David Lewis

Dear Father God, we thank you for all the books in our book corner/library. Help us to enjoy them and look after them properly.

We build our school on thee, O Lord;
  To Thee we bring our common need:
The loving heart, the helpful word,
  The tender thought, the kindly deed:
    With these, we pray,
    Thy Spirit may
Enrich and bless our school alway.[34]

This is *our* school, dear God –
Help us to make it a happy school.
  Forgive us if we are selfish or unkind;
  Forgive us if we hurt other people;
  Forgive us if ever we cause damage;
  Forgive us if we waste our time.
So help us to do our best, to be good members of our
school and to do nothing to harm our school or hurt
those around us, so that it is indeed a happy place.

O Lord, bless our school and all who work in it.

The head teacher and all the teachers, who do so much to make our work interesting and help us to learn;

The school secretary and the welfare ladies, who do many different helpful things around the school;

The dinner ladies, who cook and serve our meals and the ladies who look after us when we are playing outside;

The caretaker(s) and cleaners, who help to look after our school building and keep it clean.

Lots of people, who come into school from time to time, to keep us healthy, to tell us special things or to take assembly or special lessons.

And so many children, all different, with many lessons to learn and opportunities to work and play together.

Bless us, we pray, and help us to remember that, in our school, we are a kind of family who should all be working together happily and helping one another.

Beginning and end of term

As we come together for the first time in our new school year, O God, we ask your help and blessing throughout the year.

Help us to work as well as we can and grow in knowledge;

Help us to get to know our teachers and to make new friends;

Help us to work and play happily together;

And grant to all, teachers and children, a rewarding year.

Dear Father God, as we come together for the first time in a new school year, we ask your blessing. Help us to settle down in our new classes so that we may enjoy our learning and our friendships.

Dear God, we come to you at the beginning of our second term of the year and we ask again for your help and blessing. We know it will not be an easy term because we can expect cold weather, perhaps with ice and snow, and there always seems to be more illness about. So please help us to overcome all our difficulties and enable us to do a good term's work.

As we begin our Summer Term, O God, we look forward to nice weather and all sorts of interesting things to do – school journeys, sports, outdoor activities. Help us to enjoy all these things but also to remember that we have lots of work to do and that this is the last term in our present classes. So help us to make the most of the term that, at its end, we shall feel that it has been time well spent.

Thank you, dear God, for the short holiday we are going to have *next week*. Help us to enjoy the holiday, to be helpful at home, to do nothing that is silly and to come back afterwards refreshed and ready to settle down again to our work.

Dear God, thank you for the half-term holiday we have just enjoyed. It was nice to have a few days at home – but now we are back in school for the second half of the term and we ask you to help us to settle down to our work so that none of our time may be wasted.

Dear God, this second half of the term is only a short one and there are so many things to be done. Please help us not to waste any of the time you have given us.

Dear Father God, now that we have come to the end of the year we thank you for all we have done and ask that we may enjoy our holiday before we return for another year. For those who are going to another school after the holiday we ask a special blessing. Please be with us all, dear God.

We come together today, O God, for the last time in our present school year.
Thank you
    For lessons that have been learned and enjoyed;
    For occasions which we will remember for a long time;
    For our own special awards and achievements;
    For all those who have taught and helped us;
    For everything that has helped make it a happy year.
Upon those who are leaving today we ask your blessing and your help when they start their new schools. For those of us returning after the holiday we ask a happy holiday and a good start afterwards in our new classes. [We say thank you for all the work done by *Mr*........................ who is leaving today and ask that you will bless *him* as *he* goes to another school/retires.]

Grant, O God, that all we have learned may be remembered and that we shall use this knowledge for or own benefit, to help others and to serve you.

God, whose Name is Love,
Little ones are we!
Listen to the hymn
That we sing to thee.

Help us to be good,
Always kind and true,
In the games we play
Or the work we do.[22]

Florence Hoatson

Dear God, we know that you will be near us all day even when we are busy doing our work or playing our games. Help us to do only those things which are right and keep us from foolish or selfish behaviour.

Dear Father God, help me to learn all I can today, to work hard at my lessons and work together with others so that I can learn how to live happily and well.

Be Thou with us every day,
In our work and in our play,
When we learn and when we pray:
Hear us, holy Jesus.

Thomas Benson Pollock

A verse written on the grave of the novelist, Winifred Holtby (1898–1935) at Rudston, Yorkshire.

God give me work
Till my life shall end
And life
Till my work is done.

Heavenly Father, may what you want, be done in our school today. Help us to work hard, remembering to finish carefully the things we begin. Help us to be kind and friendly, ready to lend and give. Make us helpful in the classroom, specially when it comes to the jobs that nobody likes. Be with us in our speaking that we may say only the things that are true and good.

For Jesus' sake.[28]

Zinnia Bryan

The wisest and greatest
  In work take delight,
Whatever their hand finds
  They do with their might;
Lord, make me a worker,
  To toil with good cheer,
That earth may be better
  Because I am here.

A. Capes Tarbolton

Dear God, help us to make good use of today so that when we come to its end we may feel well satisfied with what we have done. Help us to work conscientiously, to play fairly and to be thoughtful for the feelings of others.

Dear God,
  Thank you for all my favourite times at school;
    for my favourite lessons and my favourite games;
    for being with my friends;
    for the books I enjoy reading and the quiet library;
    for the times when my teacher says, 'That's good!'
    for the pages in my book with no missings-out or mistakes;
    for bright paints and new plasticine.[28]

David Lewis

129

Thank you, God our Father for hands and all that we can do or make with them.

For pictures that we can draw, crayon or paint,
Thank you, God our Father;
For all sorts of things to make with card or paper,
Thank you, God our Father
For dolls and figures to make and dress,
Thank you, God our Father;
For plasticine and clay to use for modelling,
Thank you, God our Father;
For crafts and skills of many different kinds,
Thank you, God our Father;
For knitting and needlework, woodwork and pottery,
Thank you, God our Father.

O God, you have given us hands and brains to use to create things. Give us the skill to use them well so that we get much benefit from doing so.

O God, thank you for the interesting or exciting things we shall do today. But help us, too, to do our best in those lessons which we may not enjoy so much, remembering that it is important that we should learn these things.

Dear God, music is so important to us because we use it in so many different ways:

We sing when we are happy;
We praise you by singing our hymns;
We like to hum and make other music with our voices;
We enjoy tapping out the rhythm of a tune;
We like to dance to lively music;
Sometimes we just like to sit and listen
Or feel moved by music with a strong beat;
We may like to learn to play an instrument
And make music with other children.

Thank you, O God, for so many kinds of music and so many ways of enjoying it.

Help us, dear God, to make friends with new children who come to our school, to make them feel welcome, to invite them to join in our games and to help them to settle down in class just as we would wish others to be kind to us if we had to change school.

Dear Father God, we want to help any boys and girls at our school who are unhappy.
Some are unhappy because they are shy and lonely.
Some are unhappy because they are not feeling very well.
Some are unhappy because they have quarrelled with their best friend.
Some are unhappy because their Mummy is in hospital.
(*Add other sentences as suitable.*)
Lord, help us to be especially kind to any boys and girls who are unhappy today. Show us what we can do to make them happy.[22]

Dear God, there are some times when we are so upset by other children that we feel we want to do something to hurt them. Forgive us if we feel like that; help us to control our feelings; and remind us that even on the cross Jesus asked forgiveness for those who had hurt him so cruelly.

Dear God, there are some children in school I do not like very much:
Some of them say and do spiteful things;
Some are bossy and always want their own way;
Some will never let me play games with them;
Some have dirty habits like spitting;
Some are a nuisance in class and stop me learning;
And some . . . well, I just don't like them.
Of course, there may be some reason why other children do not like me. If so, please show me what it is and help me to do something about it.

Help, please!

Dear God, it was a bit of a rush to get to school in time this morning. I was so busy that I forgot to say 'Good morning' to you. Please excuse me and help me always to remember my morning prayer.

Dear God, when we open a book we may find lots of different things . . .
    Interesting stories . . .
    Lovely pictures . . .
    Torn pages . . .
    Grubby finger marks . . .
Our lives are like open books to you. Help us to keep them interesting, lovely and clean. May we not spoil them with unpleasantness, bad habits, or anything that would damage our future.

Dear God, sometimes we forget things that we ought not to forget:
    We forget to say 'Good morning' to people;
    Sometimes we forget to say 'Thank you';
    We may forget to be polite to others;
    We forget our good manners;
    Sometimes we even forget things on purpose
    because we do not want to do them.
Please help us not to be forgetful of such things.

Dear God, help us to put our minds to our work and give us skill as we use our hands so that we may have the pleasure of knowing that we have done our best and of seeing work well done.

Help us, O God, to do your will this day.

Dear God,
Make me honest:
Honest with others;
Honest with myself;
Honest with you;
Always.

Help me, O God,
Not to think myself more important than I am;
Not to think that I am always right;
But to see myself just as I am and as I should be.
Please teach me to be humble.

Dear God, we believe that you are able to do all things and so we place our trust in you to guard and guide us throughout this earthly life.

Dear God, you know what I am like
Better than I know myself.
So my prayer is just a simple one:
'Please help me today
In whatever way you see is best for me.'

A prayer of an African girl
O thou great Chief, light a candle within my heart that I may see what is therein and sweep the rubbish from thy dwelling place.[15]

From the Great Prayer Book of Islam, The Al-Hizbul-A'zam
O Allah (God)! keep me firm lest I should slide (from the right path) and continue to guide me lest I should go wrong.

Dear Father God, you are always watching over us even when we are not thinking about you. Please be with us when we are busy today and help us to think of you when we are able to do so.

Dear Father God, teach us the difference between right and wrong. Help us to do what is right and forgive us, please, when we do wrong.

Dear Father God, there are lots of jobs that have to be done in our classroom and we like to help teacher. If we are given jobs to do, help us to do them well. If the jobs are given to others let us not be disappointed, knowing that we have to take our turn.

Dear Father God, it is not nice to be told off for doing something wrong. So please help us only to do what is right today and to try very hard not to do anything that will hurt or upset others.

Dear Father God, we know that there are some things we may do and some things that are wrong for us. Help us to do only what is right so that we do nothing to cause trouble for us or for others.

O God, forasmuch as without thee we are not able to please thee; mercifully grant that thy Holy Spirit may in all things direct and rule our hearts; through Jesus Christ our Lord.[1]

Book of Common Prayer

God be in my head,
   and in my understanding;
God be in mine eyes,
   and in my looking;
God be in my mouth,
   and in my speaking;
God be in my heart,
   and in my thinking;
God be at mine end,
   and at my departing.

Sarum Primer

Dear God, teach us not to tell lies and even little fibs for once we start doing so it is so hard to stop. Help us always to be truthful, even when we know it may be difficult, because we know that is what you would like us to be.

Dear God, there are some times when I am tempted to take something that does not belong to me because it is something that I would like to have or cannot afford to buy. Please help me to remember that it is wrong to steal and help me to control myself if I am tempted in this way.

Dear God,
You know what today has in store for me.
Please make me thankful for all I shall enjoy
And help me to make the best of everything else.

The things, good Lord, that we pray for, give us grace to labour for.

St. Thomas More

Dear God,
Be good to me:
Thy sea is so wide,
And my boat is so small.

Breton fishermen's prayer

Dear God, give me patience. Everything does not need to happen immediately, even though I sometimes expect it to.

Dear God, if we make mistakes today, please help us to learn from those mistakes so that we do not make the same mistakes again.

Teach me, my God and King,
In all things Thee to see;
And what I do in anything,
To do it as for Thee.

George Herbert

Guard our lips, dear God, and grant that nothing may pass through them this day that is hurtful or thoughtless.

Sometimes, O God, the good work we do seems not to be noticed. When this happens, help us to remember that it is more important that we know that we have done our best.

Dear God, I know I shall need your help today,
So please stay near . . . all day.

Make me all through today, O God,
    Obedient to my parents;
    Respectful to my teachers;
    Diligent in my work;
    Fair in my games;
    Clean in my pleasure;
    Kind to those whom I can help;
    True to my friends;
    And loyal to you.
This I ask for Jesus' sake.[7]

Dr. William Barclay

Help me today, O God,
    To keep my temper and to control my tongue;
    To keep my thoughts from wandering and my mind from straying;
    To quarrel with no one and to be friends with everyone.
So bring me to the end of today with nothing to be sorry for, and with nothing left undone; through Jesus Christ my Lord.[7]

Dr. William Barclay

May the strength of God pilot us.
May the power of God preserve us.
May the wisdom of God instruct us.
May the hand of God protect us.
May the way of God direct us.
May the shield of God defend us.
May the host of God guard us against the snares of evil and the
    temptations of the world.
May Christ be with us.
Christ before us.
Christ in us.
Christ over us.
May Thy salvation, O Lord, be always ours this day and for
    evermore.

St. Patrick

School staff

We ask your blessing, O God, upon all who will be in school today – teachers, helpers, dinner ladies, the caretaker and lots of children. Please help us all to have a happy day. Help our teachers as they teach us and show us how we can be helpful to them.

Thank you, dear God, for this school and all those who teach us. Give them patience today, and help us to do nothing that would make their job of teaching us more difficult. And please be with all others who work in the school. Show us how we can be helpful to them so that we can all have a good day.

A staff retirement
Dear God, we ask your blessing today on Mr......................... who is retiring from school after working here for many years. Thank you for all the help that *he* has given to hundreds of boys and girls and the loyal service to our school. Please help *him* to have a long, healthy and happy retirement.

Death of a member of staff
Dear God, today we remember Mr......................... and we are sad that *he* has died. We remember all that *he* has done in the school for so many children, for the lessons *he* taught and the example *he* gave. Thank you for *his* life and work and for the memories that we shall keep in our hearts of happy days together. Please comfort all who mourn and help them at this time of sadness.

A staff wedding
Dear God, we are very pleased that Mr......................... is getting married and we ask that *he* may be very happy in *his* marriage. We ask you to bless *his* home and family with joy and love for many, many years.

Dear God, as we think of all that our school means to us, we say thank you for all who are responsible for it.

The members of the Education Committee

The School Governors

The Chief Education Officer and his staff

(*Church authorities*.........................)

Thank you, too, for the Head Teacher and all the school staff who give us the best education they can. Help us to show our thanks by making the most of our opportunities.

Thank you, dear God, for all those people who do things to help our school. Tonight our school governors will be meeting and we ask you to help them in any decisions they have to make so that they will do what is best for our school.

O God, we like to think of our school as a family and we are pleased that some of our parents like to be a part of our school family too. They do lots of things for us through the Parents' Association, by helping in school and going with our teachers on visits to look after us. Thank you for all people who enjoy helping our teachers and us.

Thank you, dear God, for the Parent Teacher Association of our school and for all they do to help us to have the things we need by raising money in lots of different ways.

We think today of all they are doing to buy us *a learner pool/library books/*........................ May they have much pleasure and enjoyment as they work together for our school.

Thank you, dear God, for all teachers and pupils who helped make this school what it is today, and especially those who are still interested in what we are doing. Please bless them all.

Special occasions

Dear Father God, *this afternoon/tonight* we shall be taking part in our *concert/nativity play/*........................ Thank you for the fun we have had in preparing it and thank you for those who have shown us what to do. Help us to do our best so that it will be a happy time for all who come.

Thank you, dear Father God, for giving us the chance this evening, in our concert, to show our parents and friends what we can do. Please help us to do our best.

Dear Father God, we shall be having our carol service tomorrow and some of our parents will be coming too. Please help us to have a happy time together as we praise you with our carols.

Tonight, dear God, we shall be presenting our nativity play for our parents and other visitors to see. Help us to do our best and to remember that we are not only doing a play but telling the story of how you loved us all so much that you sent Jesus to us.

Dear God, it is very nice in school sometimes to have a day that is 'different'. Today is one because........................ Please help us all to enjoy it.

Dear God, some of our children will be going out *this evening* to take part in a *music festival/*........................ with children from other schools. Please be with them, help them to do their best, to enjoy the event, and to give a lot of pleasure to all those who attend.

Prayers for Open Day

Today, dear Father God, our school will be open for our parents to come to see our work and talk to our teachers. Thank you for giving us work to do and for helping us to do it, and thank you for all our teachers and parents who have been so pleased when we have done well.

Dear God, we thank you for all the work and activities of this present school year. We are thankful for the help of many people:
    Our parents, who have encouraged us to learn;
    Our teachers, who have taught us many new things;
    Our friends, who have often worked with us;
    And many others, helping in lots of different ways.
Thank you for the opportunity today to show our work to our parents. And thank you, dear God, for all you have done for us, for your love and care and blessing.

A school fête or special event

Dear God, you know we have been working very hard to prepare for our........................ (*name the special event*) and we are looking forward to it. Thank you for all the pleasure we have had in preparing for it [the enjoyment of making things], and the fun of working with our friends. Now we pray that it may be a great success, giving pleasure both to those who take part and those who attend, making it a happy and memorable occasion for all.

Dear God, we are looking forward to our *Summer Fête/Easter Fair/May Festival* tomorrow, when we are hoping to have a lot of fun and raise money for our *school fund*. Thank you for lots of people who have helped us prepare and all those who will be very busy tomorrow. Bless all our efforts and please help us to make it an enjoyable day.

School journeys and visits

Dear God, you know we are excited because we are going to........................ today. May our excitement not cause us to do silly things.

Dear Father God, while we are out of school today, may we do nothing that would spoil the day for anyone else.

Dear God, we are looking forward today to a visit to........................ Please help us to have a good day; to look, to listen and to remember; to learn all we can from our visit; and, above all, to behave ourselves in such a way that everyone else can have a good day too.

While we are out of school today, O God, help us to remember that others will judge our school by the way we behave. Help us to be attentive to all that is said and to carry out any instructions promptly. May nothing we do spoil the day for ourselves or for others and may all we do bring credit to our school.

Today, O God, we are thinking of our friends who are going on a school journey to........................ While away, please help them
   To enjoy their time away from home and school;
   To learn many new things as they go to new places;
   To work and play happily together;
   To do nothing that is silly, dangerous or upsetting;
   To uphold the good name of our school.
And then, O God, please bring them safely home.

Dear God, thank you for the safe return of our school journey party. May they have happy memories of their time together.

Sporting occasions

When we have our sports this afternoon, dear God, please help us
> To do our best in every event we enter;
> To remember that doing our best is more important than winning;
> To avoid being big-headed if we win;
> To refrain from sulking or showing off if we lose;
> And to applaud the good efforts of others.

So, please, God, help us to have a happy time together.

Lord, help us to realise that sport is for relaxation and life won't end if the other lot win. Help us to play fairly and obey the rules, and if possible to beat the others. If we lose let us accept defeat cheerfully; keep us from being bad-tempered and spiteful, and from spoiling the enjoyment of others.[18]

Thank you, God, for a most enjoyable *sports/gala/match* last night, for the enjoyment it gave us and the successes we had. [We did not win the trophy but] we were pleased that those who entered did their best in a good sporting spirit, brought credit upon themselves and upheld the good name of our school.

O Lord, please help us to show good sportsmanship always.

After an unpleasant incident
Dear God, at our *football match/sports/*........................ yesterday, some of our children behaved very badly, showing themselves to be bad losers and giving our school a bad name. We are sorry that this happened and ask that, in future, we may all control ourselves so that this should not happen again.

O Lord,
Let your blessing
Rest upon all schools
And colleges.
To those who teach
Grant knowledge,
Patience and enthusiasm;
To those who learn
Give guidance,
Understanding, perseverance
And wisdom;
That together
They may create
A happy atmosphere
Of learning and respect
In which all may find pleasure
And your Name
May be praised.

PEOPLE AROUND US

Dear God . . .

What a lot of people there are in our world and they are all different!

Some of them mean a lot to us because they help us, or care for us, or work for us.

Some we know have problems because they are ill, or old, or lonely, disabled or in danger.

Some we shall never know because they live in other lands . . . and some are hungry or homeless.

Make us thankful for all who help us and show us how to help those who need our help.

All sorts of people

Dear God when we think of our own family we think of lots of different kinds of people. Your family is so much bigger than ours, with many more different kinds of people. But you are the great Father of all and we ask that we may behave as good members of your family.

Dear God, we look around us and see so many children who are all different. We are glad we are different because life would be very dull if we were all the same. But because we are made like this we have different likes and dislikes. Please help us to understand those who may think differently from ourselves and to remember that they have just as much right to their beliefs and thoughts as we have to ours.

Dear God, please help us not to dislike people just because they are different from ourselves. Teach us how we can learn from one another and help us to understand others better.

Dear Father God, we are very ordinary children, but we think you must have liked ordinary people because you made so many of them. Thank you for making us just as we are. Please help us to be what you would like us to be.

Dear God, you have put millions of people in the world and you have made each one different – so please help me not to think that everyone should be like me.

Dear Father of the world family, please take care of all little children everywhere. Keep them safe from danger, and help them to grow up strong and good.[4]

Dear God, some people seem to have much more than we have:
Some are clever with their hands or their brains;
Some seem to do things well without even trying;
Some may have better clothes or more possessions;
Some live in a bigger or nicer house;
But then, O God, you made us like we are, so help us not to be envious of what others may have but to make the most of what we have.

Dear God, please help us always to look beyond the outward appearance and see all people for what they are – children of God.

Dear God, thank you that, although we are so different, we are all your children. Forgive us that sometimes we judge other people by their background, their religion or the colour of their skins. Remind us that all people are equal in your sight for you are the great Father of all and we should think of each other as brothers and sisters. Help us to remember that it is not what we look like that matters but what we are. Teach us how to live together in love and peace.

Dear God, because we have come from different backgrounds, we have different names for you and we worship you in different ways. Help us to understand the beliefs of others and to know that you are the great God of us all.

Help us, dear God, to remember that all people are your children, created in your image and equal in your sight. Keep us from thinking too highly of ourselves or from looking down upon others, and show us how to live together in love and friendship because we know that you love us all.

People who care and help

While we are growing up, dear God, there are lots of times when we need someone to look after us or help us know what to do. Thank you for all those people who care for us.

Dear God, there are so many people who help us day by day that we can never count them all. Please make us thankful and help us to show our thanks by being helpful to others.

Dear God, today we are thinking of those people who are very helpful to us and we want to say *Thank you, God*.
For people who do things to help us,
Thank you, God;
For people who keep us from harm and danger,
Thank you, God;
For people who teach us and show us how to do things,
Thank you, God;
For people who comfort us when we are troubled,
Thank you, God;
For people who love us and care for us,
Thank you, God;
And for all others who help us in lots of ways,
Thank you, God.

Dear God, thank you for the lollipop man/lady who helps us to cross the road safely when we come to school and when we go home again. Help us to remember to do as he/she tells us and to say thank-you each time we are helped.

Dear Father God, our lollipop man/lady is always there, whatever the weather, to see us safely on our way to school and we would just like to say thank you for someone who is so helpful to us.

For all those people who help us day by day, thank you, God.

Dear God, there are so many books in the library that it is not always easy to find what we want or what we can read. Thank you for the librarians who work there and are so helpful to us when finding books.

Invite children to name some of the people out of school whom they find particularly helpful or caring.
Dear God, some grown-ups don't seem to like children but there are others who are so very helpful to us, people like .... (*Refer to those mentioned by the children*). Thank you for people such as these. Please show us how we, too, can be helpful, especially to younger children.

Thank you, dear God, for all those people to whom we can go for help when we need it:

For parents and other members of our family who love us and always want the best for us;

For teachers and others who help us to learn and to grow up knowing how to do the right things;

For teachers in Sunday Schools and leaders of organisations to which we belong;

For priests, ministers and others in places of worship which we attend, who help us to know you.

And for all those people we know to be friendly – policemen, shopkeepers and others – people who have helped us or our friends in the past – we say a very big Thank you, dear God.

Dear Father God, you are so great and I am so small, yet you care for me and tell me to call you Father. Thank you, Father.

People who give pleasure

Dear Father God, it is so nice to be happy and able to laugh at things. Thank you for all people who make us happy and give us pleasure.

Ask children which television programmes they enjoy most.
Dear God, thank you for television and for so many kinds of programme to watch, especially our favourite programmes such as........................

Thank you for the people who write the stories, those who produce the programmes, those who act or dance or sing and all the people who send the programmes to us through our television sets.

Dear Father God, the fair will be coming *soon*. We shall be able to enjoy the swings, the roundabouts and lots of other rides and side-shows . . . as well as candy floss, hot dogs and a chance to win prizes. It is great fun. Thank you for the showmen and fairground people who bring it to us.

Thank you, dear God, for actors and actresses who entertain us with plays and pantomines. We enjoy it when they come into school or when we can go to see them in a theatre, so we say thank you for these enjoyable times.

(Before using the following, it is suggested that a note be made of who is in the top places of the current 'Pop' music charts. Ask the children for favourites too.)
Dear God, thank you for so many kinds of music that we can enjoy. We do not all like the same kind of music but lots of people now are listening to........................ Thank you for all kinds of music and for the people who play it so that we can enjoy it.

Dear God, it is nice to have something to read. We like our comics, grown-ups like their newspapers and magazines and we all enjoy books. Thank you for those who write stories for our comics and those who draw the pictures. Thank you for editors, writers and reporters who make the newspapers and magazines. Thank you for those who write and publish books. And thank you for all those people, newsagents, booksellers and librarians who help us to get them so easily.

Dear Father God, thank you for the enjoyment of the circus and all those people who entertain us:
   The ladies in their beautiful dresses on the horses;
   The man who goes in the cage with the lions;
   The trapeze and tightrope artistes who thrill us;
   The jugglers and acrobats with their great skill;
   And the clowns who do such funny things.
Thank you, God, for circus people and their animals.

Dear God, there are lots of people who have used their talents to create things that are beautiful. Thank you for artists and craftsmen, authors and composers, poets and playwrights and all others who have enriched our lives.

Ask children to say who gives them pleasure and why – (hopefully some that are a little unusual).
Dear God, we all take pleasure in different things and we would like to thank you for those people who give us special pleasure:
   The ice-cream man, who is always so cheerful;
   The man in the corner house with his lovely dog;
   The lollipop lady who gives us a nice smile;
   Our Brown Owl who is so kind and helpful;
   .... *(add or substitute)*
Help us to show our thanks by giving pleasure to others.

People who serve

Dear Father God, we remember the people who help us by delivering things to our homes:

The postman who brings us letters and parcels;

The milkman who brings our milk every day;

The paper-boy who brings the newspapers.

(*Add others where appropriate, e.g. baker, laundry-man, coal merchant.*)

We thank you, Father God, for these people and for the work they do to help others.[22]

Dear God, on days when we like to be warm and cosy in our homes, we say thank you for people who go out, whatever the weather, and bring things to our homes:

The milkman;

The postman;

The paper boy/girl;

........................(*any others*).

Help us to appreciate what they do for us.

We think today, dear God, of those people who do dirty jobs like cleaning the streets, collecting our rubbish, or working on drains and sewers. Help them to know that they are doing important work and help us to be thankful for what they do.

Thank you, dear God, for the milkman who brings our milk no matter what the weather may be like.

Dear Father God, thank you for our village (local) policeman. It is nice to know that he is there to help us when we need him and that he helps to stop people doing wrong. Thank you, too, for all other policemen and policewomen.

Dear Father God, sometimes we see fire engines racing along the street with lights flashing and sirens sounding. We know that somewhere people are waiting anxiously for them to arrive to put out a fire. Thank you for all the brave firemen who are ready to race to work to help people in trouble.

Dear Father God, bless all the brave firemen who risk their lives when there is a fire. Please keep them free from harm and danger.

Thank you, dear God, for the ambulance men who are always ready to help people who are ill or have had accidents. It is so nice to know they are there when we need them.

Dear God, we remember today those who serve in the armed forces of our land to defend us from enemies and to try to keep peace.
Hear our prayer, O God:
    For those who serve in the army, many of them now in places where there is fighting or unrest;
        Hear our prayer, O God;
    For the officers and men of the Royal Navy, braving the dangers of the sea as well as those of an enemy,
        Hear our prayer, O God;
    For members of the Royal Air Force, ready to go into action quickly if needed,
        Hear our prayer, O God;
    For those specially trained for dangerous work – Royal Marines, Parachute Regiments and other units,
        Hear our prayer, O God.
We are thankful that there are men and women like these who are prepared to risk and even lose their lives for their country. Bless them and their families, especially when they are in dangerous situations, and keep them safe.

People at sea

Thank you, dear God, for all the sailors who bring us lots of good things from other lands. Please keep them safe when seas are rough and storm winds blow.

O God, be with all those people who go to sea:
    Sailors on passenger ships and ferries
    And those who bring us things from other lands;
    Fishermen and those who sail in small boats;
    Lifeboatmen who rescue those in danger.
Bless, too, their wives and families who wait anxiously at home especially in times of bad weather or other danger.

Dear God, when the weather is bad and strong winds are blowing, we think of people who are at sea, tossed about on angry waves and perhaps in great danger. We are thankful for all who sail the seas to bring us food and many other things we need and we ask that you will look after them when in danger and bring them safely into port.

We thank You, heavenly Father,
For the harvest of the sea;
For shining silver fishes
The fishermen bring to me.

In rain and wind and sunshine,
As they trail their long, brown nets,
The small boats leave the harbour
Just as the red sun sets.

Oh keep them safe, we pray You,
When the stormy breezes blow,
And bring them back at day-break
With fine, full nets to show.[22]

E. M. Stockham

Heavenly Father, we ask that Your protection may rest upon those who man the lifeboats along the dangerous stretches of our coasts. We pray for the wives and mothers and sisters who see their menfolk go out, never knowing if they will return. Bless the men for their courage as they risk their lives for others with no thought of reward or gain, and remind us to support them through our prayers and gifts.[16]

Beryl Bye

Thank you, dear God, for all the fishermen who put to sea in all kinds of weather to bring us the fish to eat. Be with them as they work at sea and grant them a safe return to harbour. And bless all those people in organisations such as the Mission to Deep Sea Fishermen, who do so much to help the fishermen.

Today, dear God, we think of people who help sailors around our coasts:
    Those who are responsible for lighthouses;
    Men who work on lightships;
    Coastguards who are always on the lookout;
    Lifeboatmen and the Lifeboat service;
    Helicopter pilots and rescue teams;
    Captains and crews of rescue and salvage tugs.
Thank you, God, that all these are able to help when people are in trouble or danger. Please protect them when they risk their own lives to save others.

Eternal Father, strong to save,
Whose arm doth bind the restless wave,
Who bidd'st the mighty ocean deep
Its own appointed limits keep,
O hear us when we cry to Thee
For those in peril on the sea.

William Whiting

All sorts of workers

For those who work to give us so much we enjoy, we say Thank you, God our Father.

Thank you, dear God, for all the people who serve in the shops, the grocer, the baker, the butcher, all those people in the supermarket, and lots of others who help us when we want to buy things. They are very busy people and sometimes get very tired. Help us always to be polite to them.

Thank you, dear God, for all artists, craftsmen, designers, architects and others who have helped to fill the world with so many things of beauty that we can enjoy.

Today, O God, we think of those who have worked all night whilst we have been comfortably asleep:
    Policemen, firemen and others who protect us;
    Night staff in hospitals caring for the sick;
    Miners and factory workers on the night shift;
    Drivers of trains and lorries; sailors and airmen;
    Those who produced our morning newspapers.
Grant now to all of them the rest which they need after their night's work.

> Down deep dark mines below the ground
>   Fathers and brothers toil,
> And dig for coal to warm our homes,
>   And make our kettles boil.
>
> Thank God for coal! God bless the men
>   Who work in cheerless gloom,
> And when their daily toil is done
>   God bring them safely home.[34]

C.P.

Dear God, we pray today for the people whose work is dangerous: for those who build skyscrapers, bridges, tunnels and railways; for those who knock down old buildings or cut down enormous trees; for fishermen and sailors battling with stormy seas; for soldiers and airmen; for men in factories working with powerful machines; for coal miners, spacemen and circus people; for policemen, watchmen and firemen; and for all others who are in danger through their work. Please keep them from accident, we pray. In Jesus' Name.[28]

Zinnia Bryan

Dear God, please teach all people, whatever their work may be, to take pride in their workmanship.

Dear God,
Some people have such interesting work to do:
   Some do something different nearly every day;
   Some travel to far-away countries;
   Some have lots of excitement.
Some people do jobs they like
   Such as looking after animals,
   Or helping people who are in hospital,
   Sailing ships, or playing football.
But some have dirty or dull jobs
   Like digging coal,
   Or putting tops on bottles,
   Or doing the same thing all day, every day.
Dear God, help people to enjoy their work, whatever it is, so that they may feel that they are doing something worthwhile with their lives.

God of the coalmine away under ground,
God of all workshops and wheels that go round,
God of all industry teach me to be
One of the many that labour for thee.[21]

Medical people

Dear Father God, we say thank you for all those people who help to look after us – doctors, nurses, dentists and others – and especially the ones who come into school to make sure that we are well.

Thank you, dear God, for our school nurse who does so many things for us.

For doctors and nurses, who care for us when we are not well, we say thank you, dear God.

> In times of sickness
> When we don't feel well,
> For all who care for us,
> Thank you, God.

Dear God,
Thank you for all the people who help us to get better when we are not well:
  The doctor who finds out what is wrong with us;
  The nurse who may have to give us some treatment;
  The chemist who makes up the medicine we need;
  And Mum, who gives us loving care.
Thank you for surrounding us with lots of people who care for us and want us to be well and strong.

Thank you, God, for the ambulance men and women who are always ready to help whenever they are needed. Help them when they have to make decisions so that they can do whatever is best for those they are helping.

O God, we remember before Thee the needs of those who are victims of accident and illness; we remember all hospitals and houses of healing, all chaplains, doctors, and nurses. Bless their labours in the service of their fellows, to the good of those they serve, and the greater glory of Thy holy name.[11]

A. W. Sawyer

We think today, dear God, of people who are always ready to give first aid to the injured – members of the Red Cross, the St. John Ambulance Brigade and other organisations. It is so nice to know that they are there when they are needed. Help them in their work and let them know how thankful people are for the help they give.

Dear God, there is something about dentists that we do not like. They are very nice people but we don't like it when they take out or fill our teeth. When they have to do these things to us, please give us courage and help us to know that we shall feel better afterwards.

After each sentence the response is 'O Lord, hear our prayer'.
Dear God, we thank you for hospitals to which we can go if we are ill or have an accident. Hear our prayers for those who work or are being treated in hospitals today.

For consultants, house doctors, surgeons, physicians . . . .
For all nursing staff and auxiliaries . . . .
For specialists in many departments . . . .
For orderlies, secretaries and those who keep records . . . .
For those working in casualty departments . . . .
For patients waiting for or receiving treatment . . . .

We pray, O God, that you will grant skill to all who need it, clear thinking in case of emergency and the patience and dedication needed by all who would help those in distress.

People in need

Hear our prayer, O Lord, for children in need:
    Children who have no parents or family;
    Children who have no home;
    Children who are ill or in hospital;
    Children who are starving;
    Children who cannot see or hear;
    Children who are cruelly treated.
Bless them and bless all who help them.

Today, O God, we think of children who have no parents and no home of their own. Please bless all those who run homes for homeless children and help them to make these homes happy.

Jesus, Friend of the friendless,
Helper of the poor,
Healer of the sick,
Whose life was spent in doing good,
Let us follow in Thy footsteps.
Make us strong to do right,
Gentle with the weak,
And kind to all who are in sorrow:
That we may be like Thee,
Our Lord and Master.[24]

Dear God,
We are thinking today of people who need help because they cannot look after themselves:
    Old people who have no family to look after them;
    Very ill people who cannot care for themselves;
    People who have no home of their own;
    The very poor.
Thank you for all who look after people in need [*especially
.... for whom we are raising money this year*].

Today dear God,
   We know we shall have at least one good meal;
   We shall have many interesting things to do;
   We shall enjoy books and pictures;
   We may watch television or listen to music;
   And we shall go to our comfortable homes,
   Enjoy the love of others,
   And sleep tonight in a nice cosy bed.
Hear our prayer for children in many lands who have none of
these things and keep us thankful.

Dear God, it is sad to see people in the cities who have no
homes, tramping the streets by day and sleeping outdoors at
night. We are glad that there are people and organisations that
can help and we ask you to bless the work they do.

Today, O God, we remember those unable to work:
   Those who have lost their jobs and are unemployed;
   Those who are unable to find work to do;
   Those who are sick or disabled.
O God, hear our prayer for all who suffer hardship until they
can find useful employment, and also for their families.

Dear God
When you created the world you made man in your likeness –
you made him a creator too –
always wanting to make things –
to work, to build, to do something worth doing.
So we pray for those who cannot work,
who are unemployed and have no work,
who have too much time
and too little to do in it.
Help them to make good use of time
until they can find work to do and joy in doing it.

Lord of the stable and of the hillsides, we thank You for the homes that You have given us,
   For a door to shut against the night,
   For a roof and walls to keep out the cold and rain,
   For a fire at which we can warm ourselves,
   For a table at which we can gather to eat and talk.
We pray for those who have no homes and who must live without privacy or security.
We pray for those whose only home is a crowded tenement room or a rough shelter of planks or corrugated iron.
Lord, in our comfort, remind us of the uncomfortable, in our plenty, give us concern for all those in need.[16]

Beryl Bye

As we remember people who are in need, we make the response to each sentence – *O Lord, hear our prayer.*
   For people who are ill, at home or in hospital,
      O Lord, hear our prayer;
   For people who are disabled and cannot care for themselves,
      O Lord, hear our prayer;
   For people who spend their lives in bed or in chairs,
      O Lord, hear our prayer;
   For people who are old and unable to leave their homes,
      O Lord, hear our prayer;
   For people who are lonely and have no friends,
      O Lord, hear our prayer;
   For people who are sad,
      O Lord, hear our prayer;
   For people who mourn the loss of loved ones,
      O Lord, hear our prayer;
   For people who have no home or belongings,
      O Lord, hear our prayer;
   For people who have no work and those who are poor,
      O Lord, hear our prayer.
O Lord, as we look around us, we can see so many people who are in need. Help us not only to pray for them but to do anything we can to cheer them up or make their lives a little brighter.

Lord Jesus Christ, you know what it was like to go as a refugee to Egypt and later to have nowhere to lay your head, to endure hunger in the desert and thirst upon the cross, to be badly let down by others and suffer cruelly at the hands of men. Hear our prayer for those who suffer these things today. Give hope and comfort to the refugee and the homeless; have pity upon all who are hungry or suffer pain; encourage those who feel let down or deserted. And, as you gave your life for others, may we spend our lives in helping others and serving God so that your kingdom of love on earth may reach to all mankind.

Invite the children to think of people they know who are in need and to say what the needs are (without needing to name the person).
Today, dear God, we think of people who need your help:
    Old people . . . lonely people . . .
    People in hospital . . .
    .... *(any mentioned by the children).*
As we remember them in our prayer, we ask not only that you will help them but that you will show us how we may be able to help them too.

O Lord Jesus Christ, during your life on earth you knew what it was like to suffer. Look down in your love upon all who suffer today in their minds or in their bodies and give them all the help and strength they need.

We bring before thee, O Lord, the troubles and perils of peoples and nations, the sighing of prisoners and captives, the sorrows of the bereaved, the necessities of strangers, the helplessness of the weak, the despondency of the weary, the failing powers of the aged. O Lord, draw near to each; for the sake of Jesus Christ our Lord.

St. Anselm

The disabled

Thank you, dear God, that I can do so many things:
    I can run and walk, jump or dance;
    I can make things with my hands, hold tight or feel;
    I see my family and friends around me;
    I see beautiful colours and enjoy looking at books;
    I can sing or shout, or I can talk quietly with others;
    I hear music and talking, the radio and cars in the street;
How lucky I am! Some people cannot do these things – They are crippled . . . or blind . . . or deaf . . . or dumb. Help me, please, to show my thanks for all I have by helping those who are unable to do all that I can do.

Dear God, because we can see, it is difficult for us to know what it is like to be blind. Even if we close our eyes or blindfold ourselves, we know that it is only for a short while. We pray for those who can never open their eyes and for all who help them by teaching them to do things, by printing Braille books, by putting stories on tapes and by training guide dogs, so that blind people are helped to lead a full life in spite of their blindness.

O God, please be with those people who are blind and cannot see all the things that we enjoy seeing, who cannot see where they are walking or see the traffic when they want to cross the road. As they learn to do things by feeling and listening, help them to overcome their difficulties.

Dear Father God, the world is so full of interesting sounds which we often hear without thinking about them . . . like the chimes of the ice-cream van, our favourite music on the radio or cassettes, the song of birds, children playing in the play-ground, the voices of our parents. We feel sorry for people who are deaf and hear none of these things, who live in a silent world. Please help us to be patient with them.

We think today of people who are crippled or disabled and cannot do some of the things that most other people can do. Help them to overcome their difficulties and use whatever abilities they have to lead full and useful lives.

God, our loving Father, we pray for the people who cannot live an ordinary life like us: for those who are blind or deaf or unable to move. Thank you for their bravery and cheerfulness. Please comfort and help them. Be specially near them as they struggle to do things we find easy. May they know that you love them and care for them.
In Jesus' Name.[28]

Zinnia Bryan

Hear our prayers, dear God, for people who are disabled:
    For those who must spend their lives in bed;
    For people who will never be able to walk;
    For all who no longer have arms or legs to use;
    For the seriously injured and the very ill.
In their difficulties, dear God, give them comfort, patience and help; and bless all those who care for them.

Lord, I have eyes
. . . but I do not always see:
Lord, I have ears
. . . but I do not always hear:
Lord, I have hands
. . . but they are not always used:
Lord, I have feet
. . . but they are sometimes slow to move.
Forgive me, Lord, that you have given me so much when there are others who have no sight or hearing, no hands or feet yet use what they have much better than I do to serve you and others.

An accident or disaster

Dear Father God, we are sorry to hear about the floods in......................... Please help all who have lost homes or crops and comfort all who are sad or troubled.

Dear Father God, we are very sad because people have lost their lives/homes in......................... Please be with all who need help and comfort.

Dear God, we are sad because of the......................... (*disaster*). Please help the injured, comfort those who have lost loved ones and bless all who are trying to help.

Dear God, we are thinking of those people who are trapped because of......................... Please keep them calm; please give strength to their families who await their rescue; and please help the rescue workers to reach quickly those who are trapped.

Dear God, we were very sorry to hear about the *bomb/gas/factory* explosion which killed some people and badly hurt a lot of others. Comfort all those who mourn the death of their loved ones; heal all those who have been injured; and give courage to all who are in pain. May each one have from you whatever strength and help is needed.

Dear God, thank you for rescue workers, always ready to help in times of trouble, sometimes at the risk of their own lives. Thank you, too, for emergency teams of doctors and nurses. Bless all who are working now to save lives in......................... and help them in all they are doing.

Dear God, we have heard today about an earthquake in..................... where many people have been killed and lots of others have lost their homes. Be with all those who mourn and those who suffer. Bless all who are working to help them.

Lord, today our thoughts are with those who have suffered as a result of the air (road, train) accident.
We pray for the mothers and wives and sisters of those who have died, asking that Your comfort and love will surround them.
We pray for the children left fatherless or motherless or orphaned, and for those who will care for them.
We pray for those who feel responsible for the accident, that You will sustain them.
We pray for the doctors and nurses who are caring for the injured, that their work may be inspired by Your divine compassion.
You suffered, O Lord, so we know You understand their suffering.[16]

Beryl Bye

O God, we remember before you those on whom at this time disaster has come:
Bless those whose dear ones have been killed, and those whose dear ones lost their lives in seeking to save the lives of others.
Bless those who have lost their homes, those who have seen all that they toiled for for a lifetime to build up lost in an hour.
Help us always to remember those whose job it is to risk their lives to rescue others or to keep them safe – those in the fire service, in the police service, in the medical service.
We shall forget this disaster, but we ask you always to remember those who will never forget, because life for them can never again be the same.
This we ask for your love's sake.[9]

Dr. William Barclay

The Third World

Dear God, when we think of the comforts of our homes, help us to remember children of many lands who have no home. Be with those children and help them, we pray.

Dear God, if sometimes we think we are hard done by because others have more than we have, help us then to remember those people in many parts of the world who will never have half the good things that are ours to enjoy. Make us more thankful for what we have and more thoughtful for the needs of those less fortunate than ourselves.

Dear God, it is nice to be able to go into the kitchen and get myself a piece of cake or a biscuit when I fancy one. Please help those people who *never* have a cake or a biscuit, nor even enough food to stop them being hungry. And please make me thankful for all I have.

Dear Father God, forgive us that sometimes we waste food while children in many lands are starving. Help us to be thankful for all that we have and careful not to waste it.

Respond after each sentence: 'O Lord, hear our prayer.'
O Lord, our God, we bring before you in our prayers those people in many parts of the world who suffer in ways that we can never really understand:
    For people who are always starving . . . .
    And those in lands where harvests have failed . . . .
    For people who do not have even the simplest home . . . .
    And those whose homes have been destroyed . . . .
    For those who live in fear of their rulers . . . .
    And any who are unjustly imprisoned . . . .
    For all who are distressed . . . . *'O Lord, hear our prayer.'*

Lord, often we say 'I'm hungry!' and pick up a biscuit, or a packet of crisps, or some sweets. Help us to understand what it feels like to be hungry and to have nothing to eat.

We pray for those who try to help hungry people, by sharing their skills, knowledge and tools.

Help us to share what we have, so that everyone may have food to eat.[22]

A prayer of an African Christian
O Lord,
our meal is steaming before us
and it smells very good.
The water is clear and fresh.
We are happy and satisfied.
But now we must think of our sisters
and brothers all over the world
who have nothing to eat
and only a little to drink.
Please, please, let them have enough to eat
and enough to drink.
That is most important.
But give them also
what they need every day
in order to get through in this life.
Just as you have given enough to eat and drink
to the people of Israel in the desert
please give it also to our hungry and thirsty brothers,
now and at anytime.[18]

Dear God, when we see pictures of starving or homeless people in many parts of the world we feel very sad. We sometimes feel very uncomfortable, too, because we have so much whilst they have so little, yet there seems so little we can do. We can only ask that you make us generous in our giving and the leaders of the world more ready to share what they have with the poorer countries.

Lord of the loving heart,
May mine be loving too.
Lord of the gentle hands,
May mine be gentle too.
Lord of the willing feet,
May mine be willing too.
So may I grow more like to thee
In all I say and do.[5]

Dear God, even if I am tired, help me never to be too tired to help someone who needs me.

Today, dear God,
Let my hands be useful
As I do what I can
To help other people,
Doing those things
You would wish me to do.

Jesus' hands were kind hands, doing good to all,
Healing pain and sickness, blessing children small;
Washing tired feet, and saving those who fall;
Jesu's hands were kind hands, doing good to all.

Take my hands, Lord Jesus, let them work for You,
Make them strong and gentle, kind in all I do;
Let me watch You, Jesus, till I'm gentle too,
Till my hands are kind hands, quick to work for You.[34]

Margaret Cropper

O Lord, let us not live to be useless, for Christ's sake.

John Wesley

Dear God, when I think of all the sad, lonely or needy people around me, I think how much I have and am grateful. Teach me to be happy, cheerful and kind to those who are in need so that I can help to make their lives a little brighter.

Dear Father God, as we look forward to a happy Christmas, we think of people who may not have one. Please show us how we can help them.

Dear God, thank you for all the good things you have given us. You have taught us that we can best show our thanks by doing things for other people. So, please open our eyes so that we can see who needs help and then show us ways of helping.

Thank you, dear God, for organisations such as the Red Cross and the Salvation Army that are always ready to help people in time of trouble and provide many forms of service. Bless all the work they do and all who give money so that they can do it.

Dear Father God, help us as we try to get money for...................... and show those to whom we send it how best to use it.

Dear God, there are so many people in the world who need help that we find it difficult to know who we should try to help, but we have decided to try to raise money for......................
Help us in our efforts to do this so that we shall be able to send a large gift for the work that they do. Bless those who are responsible for running *the organisation* and help them to use the money wisely for those who need it.

If I can do some good today,
If I can serve along life's way,
If I can something helpful say,
Lord, show me how.

If I can right a human wrong,
If I can help to make one strong,
If I can cheer with smile or song,
Lord, show me how.

If I can aid one in distress,
If I can make a burden less,
If I can spread more happiness,
Lord, show me how.[7]

Grenville Kleiser

CHURCH AND RELIGION

Lord . . .
You live in all;
You are all;
You assume all forms;
You are the origin of all;
You are the soul of all;
All praise be to you.

(Based on a Hindu prayer from the Vishnu
Purana, these thoughts are at the heart
of all religion and worship)

The Christian Church

I believe in God, the Father Almighty, Creator of all things, who sent his Son to be the Saviour of the world.

I believe in Jesus Christ, Son of God, who died so that our sins might be forgiven, rose again from the dead, ascended into heaven and lives today.

I believe in the Holy Spirit, sent by God to those who ask, to help our understanding, guide our thoughts and actions and give us power from God.

Dear God, if my faith ever grows weak, please help me to overcome my doubts and know that you, my Father, can be my guide and strength all my days.

Thank you, God, for your love in sending your Son, Jesus. Thank you for his earthly life and teachings. Thank you that he died so that our sins could be forgiven. Thank you that he rose again and lives for ever. Thank you, God, for Jesus.

O Lord Jesus Christ, bless the work of your Church on earth until the whole world has become your Kingdom.

O Lord, convert the world – and begin with me.[35]

A Chinese Student's Prayer

Confirmation
Almighty God, who taught us through your Son Jesus that we should, through baptism, show our desire to be changed and lead a new life, we thank you for those whose parents brought them to you as children and who now wish to confirm that action by offering themselves to you for your blessing. Fill them with your Holy Spirit so that they may be guided aright and inspired to serve you faithfully all their days: in the Name of the Father and of the Son and of the Holy Ghost.

Dear God, we thank you for those people who carried out the command of Jesus to teach all people of all lands about you, and especially those who brought your word to our land. May that work continue until all people everywhere have come to learn of you and live in your ways.

Thank you, dear God, for men and women of the past who took your Good News to people all over the world. Thank you for those who carried on their work and for the churches that were formed. Thank you for people in many lands today who form your world-wide Christian Church. Bless all the churches in what they are doing and bless all in this and other lands who help provide money or encouragement for their work.

We thank you, dear God, that there are many different kinds of Christian church, so we are able to worship you in the way that *we* find best. Forgive us if sometimes we think that ours is the best or the only way to worship you; and help us to know that what is best for us may not be for someone else. May we learn from each other and work with each other for your glory.

O God, please bless the work of the World Council of Churches and of all the councils of churches in our own land, that people who worship you in differing ways may work together to help all people to get to know you better.

Let us pray for the Churches throughout the world, for their truth, unity and stability; that in all, charity may flourish, and truth may live. For our own Church, that what is lacking may be supplied, and what is unsound corrected; for the sake of Jesus Christ, our only Lord and Saviour.

Bishop Lancelot Andrewes

Worship and prayer

Thank you, dear God, for making Sunday a special day that is different from all the other days of the week, a day when most people do not have to work but can enjoy a restful day with their families.

But thank you, too, that it is your special day, when we can go to church with our families and our friends to worship you and to learn of you in the church service or our Sunday school.

Please help us when we go to give you our best in our worship, to learn from your word and from those who teach it to us and help us to understand how, in a very special way, we can meet with you in your house.

Come to us today, O Holy Spirit of God.
Help us to understand the truth about God;
Help us to live as he would have us to live;
Help us in our singing that we may praise him;
Help us to know how to pray and what to pray for;
Give us understanding as we read our Bibles;
And fill our hearts and lives with love and joy.

The great prayer of the Christian Church, the Lord's Prayer, taught by Jesus to his disciples, is offered in most services.

Our Father, who art in heaven,
Hallowed be thy Name;
Thy kingdom come.
Thy will be done on earth,
As it is in heaven.
Give us this day our daily bread.
And forgive us our trespasses,
As we forgive those who trespass against us.
And lead us not into temptation,
But deliver us from evil.
For thine is the kingdom,
The power, and the glory,
For ever and ever.

Dear Father God, teach us how to pray, so that we can 'have a word' with you just as easily as we can with our friends.

Dear Father God, sometimes we have forgotten to say thank-you when you have answered our prayers. Please forgive us and help us to be more thankful in future.

> Dear God,
> When we say our prayers
> We cannot see you.
> It is rather like talking
> To someone on the telephone.
> But when we make a 'phone call
> We don't talk all the time –
> We need to listen as well.
> Teach us, dear God,
> That prayer is not just talking:
> It is listening too.
> Teach us, when we pray, to listen
> To what you have to say to us.
> And, by the way, dear God,
> Thank you that you are always there
> When we want to get through to you.

Dear God, we do not know how you can hear so many people who are talking to you at the same time, but you are God and you listen to all our prayers. So please hear us now; help us to know how to pray and what to pray for; and answer our prayers in whatever way you know is right.

Dear God, I don't really need to say anything because you know what I am thinking and what I would ask for. So please give me whatever help you know I need.

Our church and Sunday school

Dear Father God, thank you for our church and Sunday school and for all the people we meet here week by week . . . and thank you for being with us.

Dear God, thank you for our church where we can meet for worship, to sing our hymns, to offer our prayers and to learn from your word. Help us to remember that it is your house. When we enter, may we do so quietly so as not to disturb the thoughts of others and help us to understand that, although we cannot see you, you are there to hear us and to help us.

Dear God, our church is not just a building but a group of people who want to worship and serve you as best they may. Make us into useful members of our church.

O God, please bless all who work for you in our church:
 The *vicar/minister/priest* who leads our worship;
 The Sunday School Superintendent and teachers;
 The leaders of clubs and organisations;
 The organist, choirmaster and choir;
 Those who clean the church or arrange the flowers:
 For these and........................ (*others*) we thank you.

Dear God, we ask you to bless our Sunday School. Thank you
 For those who started it many years ago;
 For the teachers who have taught in it;
 And the many children who have learned about you here;
 For the teachers who teach here week by week
 And the children who come here now.
Bless all that is done here in your Name and help us to learn how best to please you, to love you, and to serve you.

Clubs and organisations

Thank you, dear God, for clubs that we can go to after school to enjoy ourselves with other boys and girls. Be with our club leaders and helpers who do all they can to make our club evening such an interesting and enjoyable one.

Thank you, dear God, for youth organisations – Boys Brigade, Girls Brigade, Scouts, Guides, Campaigners and others – to which we can belong. Thank you for all the fun we can have and for all that we can learn as we work and enjoy ourselves with others. And thank you, dear God, for all the leaders who give their time freely to help boys and girls to grow up to lead good and useful lives.

Dear God, it is good to belong to an organisation and wear a uniform. We enjoy our evenings with others and we do all sorts of interesting things. Thank you for those who founded our organisation(s) and those who have continued their work so that children in many parts of the world can enjoy doing things just as we can.

Dear Father God, when people see us wearing our uniform they expect a lot of us. Help us never to let down our organisation, our leaders or you.

At a meeting of a youth organisation
Dear God, thank you for our *Brownie Guides/Boys' Brigade/* ...., for those who run it and all who meet with us as members. Help us all to work and play happily together, enjoying many activities and earning our badges or awards. Make us proud to wear our uniforms, loyal to our *company/pack/* ...., helpful to our leaders, friendly toward one another and true to our God.

As we read your word, dear God,
Let your Holy Spirit guide us.
Please help us to study,
To think deeply
And to understand.
Help us to discover
Any message you have for us today.
And then . . . please help us
To remember your words
And act upon them
Because that is what you want us to do.

Dear Father God, thank you for my Bible and all that it tells me about you. As I read it, help me to understand what I am reading so that I may know you better.

Dear Father God, help us to treasure our Bible because it is your word. Give us understanding as we read it so that we may learn more of you and know how you would have us to live.

Dear God, thank you for the Bible –
The word that you yourself have given us.
Thank you
   For prophets and teachers who gave the word;
   For those who gave us the Bible in our own language;
   For people who translate it for others today;
   For the great work done by the Bible Societies;
   For those who prepare notes for Bible study
   And those who teach the scriptures to others.
Help us
   Never to neglect the study of our Bible,
   But to discover the truths contained in it,
   So that we grow nearer to you.

For Thy holy book we thank Thee;
May its message be our guide,
May we understand the wisdom
Of the laws it will provide,
And Thy love and tender care
For Thy people everywhere.[34]

Ruth Carter

Dear Father God, there are some things we take for granted because they are always there. Our Bible is one of these – a real treasure chest into which we often fail to look. We think of people in many lands who would dearly love to have a Bible but cannot. Forgive us that so often we neglect to read your word.

Let your word, O God, be the light that shows us the way to the joys of your Kingdom.

Dear Father God, there are lots of people who have helped others to know you.
  There were the prophets of old.
  There was our Lord Jesus Christ.
  There were those who became his disciples.
We can read in our Bibles what they had to say, and so we say thank you for our Bibles. Help us to make time to read them often; and help us to understand what we read.

Dear God, you have given the Holy Scriptures for the guidance of all people that they may come to know you and your ways. As we read, help us to understand and make us ready to live according to what your words tell us so that we may grow nearer to you each day.

God make my life a little light
Within the world to glow;
A little flame that burneth bright,
Wherever I may go.

Matilda Betham-Edwards

Dear Father God, if at times the light that can shine in our lives seems so very small, remind us that each light is but one of many that can bring cheer into a world of darkness.

Our candles remind us, dear God
Of Jesus, your Son, the Light of the World,
In Advent the candles remind of his coming;
At Candlemas we think of the one who came
To be a light to his people but also to all peoples.
Let his light come into our lives, dear God,
And help us to shine brightly for him.

A Jewish prayer

We praise you,
O Lord our God,
King of the universe,
Maker of light
and Creator of darkness,
Giver of peace
and Creator of all things.
In your mercy
you give light to the earth
and to all who dwell in it,
and in your goodness
you renew the work of creation
continually, day by day.
We praise you, O Lord,
Creator of Light.[30]

Dear God, just as a mirror reflects the light of the sun, so may our lives reflect your love and bring some sunshine into our world.

Kindle a flame within us, O God,
That no power on earth can ever put out.

A Hindu prayer (Sivastotra, 3. adapted.)
In the darkness that is all around us and prevents us from seeing, O Lord, just rise like the sun and chase away the darkness with your divine light.

O God,
Let your light of love
Shine in this world of darkness,
So that all people may see their way
As they journey through this world,
And find the true path
That leads to the world beyond.

May the Lord Jesus Christ, who is the splendour of the eternal light, remove from our hearts all darkness now and for evermore.*

Christ is the morning star
Who, when the darkness of this world is past,
Brings to his saints
The promise of the light of life
And opens everlasting day.

The Venerable Bede

Prayers from the East

This, one of the best known Hindu prayers, is often heard during temple services:

> From falsehood lead me to the truth.
> From darkness lead me to the light.
> From death lead me to everlasting life.

A Hindu prayer from the Rig Veda

> O God, the Lord of power and might;
> Strong in your friendship we have no fear.

A prayer of the Hindu mystic poet Chaitanya (16th C.)

I do not pray for wealth, I do not pray for honours, I do not pray for pleasures or even for the joys of poetry. I only pray that during my lifetime I may have love: that I may have a pure love to love You.

Two Sikh prayers

I come to take refuge with the Lord;

    May the Divine Guru out of his mercy grant that the passions of lust, anger, greed, pride and undue attachment in me may vanish and leave me in peace.[11]

Sukhmanu 6

> There is One God,
> He is the Supreme Truth,
> He, the Creator, is without fear
> And without hate.
> He, the Omnipresent, pervades the Universe,
> He is not born, nor does He die to be born again.
> True in the beginning, true throughout the ages,
> True even now, and forever shall be true.[11]

Japji (Mool Mantra)

Two Shinto prayers of Bunjiro (founder of the Konko-Kyo sect)
God has no voice, his form is unseen. With Him there is neither night nor day, neither far nor near. Pray to Him simply, with a heart of faith. He is your friend.[11]

Give us a faith which makes us friends of Thee, O God, not a faith that makes us afraid. In faith may we come near to Thee.[11]

Some Zoroastrian (Parsi) prayers
You are one and the same God, pleased and displeased by the same things for ever.

This is a part of the prayer offered in the Naojote ceremony when a child is initiated into the Zoroastrian faith.
Help me, Lord, to do the good work I have set out to do. I want no reward or gain. All I need is the help of Your Good Mind, and Faith to get divine knowledge to spread Your word.

Here is a prayer of Zoroaster, founder of the Zoroastrian faith, in which he praises God by asking questions to which he already knows the answers (Yasna 45)
This I ask thee, tell me truly, Lord. Who in the beginning, at creation, was Father of Order? Who established the course of sun and stars? Through whom does the moon wax then wane? . . . Who has upheld the earth from below, and the heavens from falling? Who sustains the waters and plants? Who harnessed swift steeds to wind and clouds? What craftsman created both sleep and activity? Through whom exists dawn, noon and eve? . . .[17]

The following prayers are adapted from the Qur'an, the Holy Book of Islam (c. 610 CE)

This is the opening prayer (from Sura 1), repeated many times by Muslims in their daily prayers. Muslims are expected to pray five times daily.

In the name of God (*Allah*), the Compassionate, the Merciful.
Praise be to God,
The Lord of all creation,
The Compassionate, the Merciful;
Ruler of the Judgement Day!
We worship only you and pray to you for help.
Guide us in the straight way,
The way of those whom you have favoured,
Not the way of those who have made you angry,
Nor of those who have gone astray.

A prayer from Sura 34:
In the name of God (*Allah*), the Compassionate, the Merciful.
Praise be to God,
To whom all things in heaven and on earth belong!
Praise be to him for evermore;
He is full of wisdom and he knows everything.
He knows all that goes into the earth
And all that springs from it;
All that comes down from the sky
And all that goes up to it.
God is forgiving and merciful.

From Sura 114, the final chapter of the Qur'an:
In the name of God (*Allah*), the Compassionate, the Merciful.
I seek safety with the Lord of men,
The King of men, the God (or Judge) of men,
From the mischief of the evil one
Who whispers in the hearts of men.

From Sura 93:
In the name of God (*Allah*), the Compassionate, the Merciful.
By the light of day and at nightfall, your Lord has not forgotten
you, nor is he displeased with you. The life that is to come
holds a brighter future for you than the present life, You will be
well pleased with what your Lord will give you.
    Did he not find you as an orphan and give you shelter?
    Did he not find you lost and guide you?
    Did he not find you poor and take away your need?
So do not treat the orphan badly,
Nor refuse to help the beggar:
But speak out to tell the goodness of the Lord.

Also adapted from the Qur'an:
I will sound your praises, Lord of heaven and earth, when I get
up in the morning: and I will praise you in the night-time and
when the stars begin to disappear.

Part of a prayer of Muhammad for a particular matter
You are the Great Knower of unseen things, O God! If you
know that this thing is good for me in the matter of my religion
and my living . . . make it easy for me and bless me therein; and
if you know it to be evil for me . . ., then turn it away from me
and me from it. Grant to me what is good for me . . . and make
me contented with it.

The Bedouin camel drivers' prayer at sunset:
O Lord, be gracious unto us! In all that we hear or see, in all
that we say or do, be gracious unto us. I ask pardon of the
Great God. I ask pardon at the sunset, when every sinner turns
to him. Now and forever I ask pardon of God. O Lord, cover us
from our sins, guard our children and protect our weaker
friends.

From the Shih Ching, the Confucian Book of Odes, c. 800 BCE

May Heaven guard you and keep you
In comfort and safety,
In health and strength,
Giving you every blessing,
Giving you good fortune
And giving you wealth.
May Heaven guard you and keep you,
Making your crops grow well,
And sending you nothing but good,
May Heaven send down a hundred favours
And so many blessings
That the day is not long enough for them all.

WORSHIP AND THANKSGIVING

We all, verily, worship God.
We all, verily, bow down before God.
We all, verily, are devoted unto God.
We all, verily, give praise unto God.
We all, verily, yield thanks unto God.
There is none other God but Thee,
the One, the Single,
the Powerful, the Omniscient,
the Bountiful.[2]

Bahá'u'lláh (Bahái)

> May my words and my thoughts be acceptable to you,
> O Lord, my refuge and my redeemer![3]
>
> *Psalm 19; v. 14*

Dear God, you are so great but you are also our Father. Thank you for all your love for us. Help us to show our thanks by doing what we know you would like us to do.

Dear God,
I think it is wonderful that you can be everywhere and know everything. Thank you for being *my* God.

Dear God, we call you Father because you love each one of us with a very special love.
   You are glad when we are glad.
   You are sad when we are sad.
   You love us even when we behave badly.
A Father does all these things.
Thank you, God, for being our Father.[22]

> We thank You, loving Father,
> For all Your tender care,
> For food and clothes and shelter,
> And all Your world so fair.
>
> *Anon.*

Dear God, you must be very great and very clever to have made our world and it is nice to know that you have never changed since the world began. We praise and thank you because you are such a wonderful God and always will be.

Dear God,
I think about the world you created;
I think about your love for people;
. . . and I think you're *great*!

Dear God,
I'm going to close my eyes and think about you. I think it's better to close my eyes, then I can't see my toys or my books or out of the window, and it's easier to think just about you.

I don't know how you can listen to hundreds of people talking to you all at the same time, all over the world, but thank you that you can, and that you're listening to me now.[28]

David Lewis

Dear God,
I'm not going to say anything for a minute – I just want to be near you and feel safe and think about how much you love me. I am glad that I am special to you. Sometimes when I think of you, you seem very great and far away. But I know that really you are very close beside me. So now I am just going to whisper! Thank you that I don't have to shout to make you hear me.[28]

David Lewis

Please God take care of yourself –
'cos we'd be sunk without you![12]

G. Williams

Dear God, please be my guardian.
Stay near and help me
All through today and every day.

Father God, our gifts we bring
With our love today.
Bless us in the songs we sing,
And the prayers we say.

Anon.

Dear Father God, you are so great and we are so small but we worship you with our words and our music because we know you like to hear us.

Thank you, dear God, for being such a wonderful God and for giving us our world to enjoy; and thank you for helping us to know that we are your children and can call you our Father. Thank you, God, for everything.

Father, we thank You for the night,
And for the pleasant morning light;
For rest and food and loving care,
And all that makes the day so fair.

Help us to do the things we should,
To be to others kind and good;
In all we do, in work and play,
To grow more loving every day.[22]

Rebecca J. Weston

Dear Lord Jesus, thank you for listening to me when I pray to you. Thank you for loving me, helping me and teaching me every day wherever I am. I cannot see you, so please help me to know you are near me all the time, even when I am not thinking about you.

Dear Father God
As we sing, accept our praise;
As we pray, hear our prayers;
As we read your word, help us to understand;
As we listen, help us to learn of you;
As we meet together for worship, bless us;
And help us to know that we have met with you.

Dear God, we come to you at the beginning of our day to praise you for your greatness and thank you for all your gifts. Accept our praise and thanksgiving for Jesus' sake.

We praise and worship you this morning, O God:
We praise you because you are our great God;
We praise you for your love in sending Jesus;
We praise you because we can call you Father;
We praise you for every blessing you give us.
With all we have, we praise you, O God.

Almighty God, whose glory the heavens are telling, the earth thy power, and the sea thy might, and whose greatness all feeling and thinking creatures everywhere herald: to thee belongeth glory, honour, might, greatness and magnificence now and for ever, to the ages of ages; through Jesus Christ our Lord.

Liturgy of St. James (2nd C.)

Holy, Holy, Holy,
Lord God of hosts;
Heaven and earth are full of Thy glory;
Glory be to Thee, O Lord most High.[1]

Book of Common Prayer

In our morning prayers, dear God, help us to bring to you not only our words but ourselves. Teach us how to pray and what to pray for, remembering the needs of others before we think of our own.

> Almighty God, we offer you our worship and praise,
> For you are the great Creator of all things
> And the giver of life itself;
> In your great love you sent your Son
> To be the Saviour of the world;
> And you send the power of your Holy Spirit
> To strengthen, guide and help your people:
> To you, O God, Father, Son and Holy Spirit,
> Be all honour and glory, now and for evermore.

Dear God, as we come before you now, we do not know how you can take notice of so many of us and listen not only to us but to other children in other places. But you are God and you can do anything, so please help us not to wonder *how* you can hear us but just to know that you can and you do. So, dear God, please accept our praise, hear our prayers and bless us because we trust in you.

Dear God we come to you to worship because you are so great.
　We cannot understand how you made all the world;
　We cannot tell what you are really like;
　We cannot find words to describe you;
But we do believe that you are greater than anyone else;
We do know that you loved us so much that you sent Jesus;
And we do know that he told us to call you Father.
　So we come as your children;
　We say 'Thank-you, Father';
　and we offer you the best of our praises.

Lord, we focus our eyes on you.
You are love and wisdom.
You are rest and peace.
You are joy and gladness.
You are all our riches.
You are our haven of hope, our great consolation.
You are eternal life,
Great and wonderful Lord
God Almighty
Merciful saviour.

Francis of Assisi

As we gather before you in worship, O God, help us to put all other things out of our minds so that we may truly worship you and praise you as best we are able, for you are a great and wonderful God . . . and our Father.

I will proclaim your greatness, my God and king;
I will thank you for ever and ever.
Every day I will thank you;
I will praise you for ever and ever.
The Lord is great and is to be highly praised;
His greatness is beyond understanding.[3]

Psalm 145; 1–3

Lord God, You are great and powerful, glorious,
splendid, and majestic. Everything in heaven and
earth is yours, and you are king, supreme ruler
over all. All riches and wealth come from you;
you rule everything by your strength and power;
and you are able to make anyone great and strong.
Now, our God, we give you thanks, and we praise
your glorious name.[3]

1 Chronicles 29; 10–13

195

Dear God, whenever we bring something to you, we have something to take away, and the more we offer to you, the more you give to us. Help us to offer our best in our worship so that we may take with us as we go a special blessing from you.

Dear God, give me the kind of faith and trust in you that tells me you can do anything – which you can!

> Now thank we all our God,
>   With hearts and hands and voices;
> Who wondrous things hath done,
>   In whom His world rejoices;
> Who, from our mothers' arms,
>   Hath blessed us on our way
> With countless gifts of love,
>   And still is ours today.

Martin Rinkart (tr. Catherine Winkworth)

Two Muslim prayers
O God (*Allah*)! whatever good thing has been received by me or any one of your creatures this morning has come only from you. You are the only God and have no partner; so all praise and gratitude is due to you.

God is greater than all else. Glory and praise to Thee, O God. Blessed is Thy Name, and exalted is Thy Majesty. There is no one worthy of worship and service but Thee.
    God is greater than all else. Glory be to God, the Exalted. God accepts him who is grateful to Him. O our God, all praise be unto Thee. God is greater than all else.
    Glory to my Lord, the most High. God is greater than all else.[11]

The Amidah, referred to in the Talmud as THE prayer, is recited standing at each of the three Jewish daily prayers.
O Lord, open my lips and let me praise you.

We bless you, O Lord our God and God of our fathers, the God of Abraham, Isaac and Jacob, the great and mighty God on high. You bestow your kind favours on us, and all things belong to you; you remember the good deeds of our fore-fathers, and in your love for them you will bring their descendants a redeemer for your name's sake.[31]

Three Jewish prayers, which form part of the morning service
May your name, O king, be praised for ever, O God and king, you are great and holy in heaven and on earth. For song and praise and reverence are yours by right, O Lord our God and God of our fathers, and so are power, supremacy and rule, greatness, might and glory, holiness, dominion, blessings and thanks now and for ever. We bless you, Lord, and praise you, great God and king. For you are the God of thanksgiving and the Lord of wonders, and you delight in songs of praise, God and king and source of all life.[31]

We thank you, for you are the Lord our God and the God of our fathers for ever. You are the rock of our lives and the shield that protects us in every generation. We thank you and praise you for our lives which are in your care, and for our souls which are in your charge, and for all the wonderful things and all the marvellous benefits that we enjoy every minute of every day, morning, noon and night. You are all goodness, your mercy never fails; you are all kindness, your favours never cease. You are always the centre of our hopes.[31]

We bless you, O Lord our God, king of the universe, for creating light and darkness, for bringing peace and for making everything.[31]

Closing prayers

Dear Father God, as we leave to go to our classes, we ask that you will go with us and stay with us all day.

Thank you, God, for listening to our songs and our prayers. We ask one more thing: 'Please stay with us all day.'

> Be near me, Lord Jesus; I ask Thee to stay
> Close by me for ever, and love me, I pray.
> Bless all the dear children in Thy tender care,
> And fit us for heaven, to live with Thee there.
>
> *Anon.*

Dear Father God, please bless us all to-day. Bless our work and our play; bless our singing and our story time; bless....................... (*whatever other activities are proposed*). Help us to do what is right today, so that we may make You happy; for Jesus' sake.[4]

> Dear God, help us throughout today:
> To work and play as well as we can;
> To be kind and helpful to all we meet;
> To say and do nothing we know to be wrong;
> And to remember that we are your children.

> Dear Father, keep me through this day
> Obedient, kind and true:
> That, always loving Thee, I may
> Seek all Thy will to do.
> Seek all Thy will to do.[24]
>
> *G. W. Briggs*

Dear God, may this time spent with you make us more ready to use today as you would have us use it.

Dear Lord Jesus, we shall have this day only once; before it is gone, help us to do all the good we can, so that today is not a wasted day. For your Name's sake.[24]

O God, forasmuch as without thee we are not able to please thee; mercifully grant that thy Holy Spirit may in all things direct and rule our hearts; through Jesus Christ our Lord.*

> Fill thou my life, O Lord my God,
> In every part with praise,
> That my whole being may proclaim
> Thy being and thy ways.
>
> *H. Bonar*

O Lord, support us all the day long of this troublous life, until the shadows lengthen and the evening comes, and the busy world is hushed, and the fever of life is over, and our work is done. Then, Lord, in thy mercy, grant us a safe lodging, a holy rest, and peace at the last.

Used by Cardinal Newman but probably 16th C.

Into thy hands, O God, we commend ourselves this day; let thy presence be with us to its close. Enable us to feel that in doing our work we are doing thy will, and that in serving others we are serving thee; through Jesus Christ our Lord.[32]

Prayers in use at Uppingham School

God watches o'er us all the day
At home, at school and at our play;
And when the sun has left the skies
He watches with a million eyes.[34]

Gabriel Setoun

Lord, keep us safe this night,
Secure from all our fears;
May angels guard us while we sleep,
Till morning light appears.*

Dear Father God, before we go home we want to say thank you for a happy day and for all those who have helped to make it happy for us.

Dear God, be with us as we go to our homes; keep us safe as we go; give us a happy evening with our families and a good night's sleep.

Glory to Thee, my God, this night,
For all the blessings of the light;
Keep me, O keep me, King of Kings,
Beneath thine own almighty wings.

Thomas Ken

A prayer of Epictetus (Stoic) adapted
When I have shut my door and darkened my room let me not say that I am alone. You, God, are with me, and need no light to see what I do.[11]

Forgive me, O God, for anyone whom I have hurt, or failed, or disappointed today, and for any wrong thing I have said or done today.

Thank you for all the new things I have learned today and for all the things I have enjoyed today.

Give me a good night's sleep tonight, and grant that tomorrow morning I may waken refreshed for work and for play. This I ask for Jesus' sake.[7]

Dr. William Barclay

Lighten our darkness, we beseech thee, O Lord; and by thy great mercy defend us from all perils and dangers of this night; for the love of thy only Son, our Saviour, Jesus Christ.[1]

At the close of the day, dear God, we come to offer our thanks.
   Thanks for so much that has helped to 'make our day';
   Thanks for new things learned and those who taught us;
   Thanks for new friendships formed and old ones enjoyed;
   Thanks for health, and food, and books, and television
   – and for everyday things we so often take for granted.
Forgive us if we have misused today, or wasted our time, if we have hurt others or failed to control ourselves; and help us to try to do better tomorrow.

Dear Father God,
   We have had a happy day together at school today.
   We have done lots of work and learned many new things.
   We have enjoyed playing together.
   Now it is time for us to go home, and we want to thank you
      for our happy day.
   Thank you, Father God!
   Thank you, Father God! (*said by the children*)[22]

May the Lord bless you and take care of you;
May the Lord be kind and gracious to you;
May the Lord look on you with favour and
give you peace.[3]

May the blessing of God the Father, God the Son, and God the Holy Spirit be with us now and for evermore.*

May God bless us and keep us, and all whom we love, in his fatherly care, now and throughout the night.

May God the Father of our Lord Jesus Christ, bless, direct and keep us, and give us thankful hearts, now and always.*

May the Lord grant us his blessing and fill our hearts with his spirit of truth and peace now and for evermore.

May the blessing of God Almighty, the Father, the Son and the Holy Spirit, rest upon us and upon all God's people everywhere, now and for ever.*

The peace of God, which passeth all understanding, keep your hearts and minds through Christ Jesus.*

The grace of the Lord Jesus Christ, the love of God, and the fellowship of the Holy Spirit be with us all, evermore.*

May God the Father bless us.
May Christ the Son take care of us.
The Holy Ghost enlighten us all the days of our life.
The Lord be our defender and keeper of body and soul both now and forever.

Bishop Aedelward

Go forth into the world in peace;
Be of good courage;
Hold fast that which is good;
Render to no man evil for evil;
Strengthen the faint-hearted;
Support the weak;
Help the afflicted;
Honour all men;
Love and serve the Lord,
Rejoicing in the power of the Holy Spirit.
And the blessing of God Almighty
The Father, the Son, and the Holy Ghost,
Be upon us and remain with us for ever.*

To the eternal King, immortal and invisible, the only God – to him be honour and glory for ever and ever![3]

May the grace of Christ our Saviour,
   And the Father's boundless love,
With the Holy Spirit's favour,
   Rest upon us from above.

Thus may we abide in union
   With each other and the Lord,
And possess, in sweet communion,
   Joys which earth cannot afford.

John Newton

Thank you for the world so sweet,
Thank you for the food we eat;
Thank you for the birds that sing,
Thank you, God, for everything.

Edith Leatham

For every cup and plateful,
God make us truly grateful.[8]

A. S. J. Fisher

For colours in the food we eat,
For smells that smell so good,
For things to taste and things to see,
For Mummy and Daddy
And for Thee,
Father in Heaven, we thank Thee.[12]

Catherine Marshall

For food to eat and those who prepare it;
For health to enjoy it and friends to share it;
Thank you, Heavenly Father.*

Dear Father, for our daily food
And giving us so much that's good,
Accept our thanks we humbly pray –
And keep us thankful day by day.

To God who gives our daily bread
A thankful song we'll raise,
And pray that he who sends our food
Will fill our hearts with praise.*

O God, by whom we all are fed,
Give us this day our daily bread.

For good food and hearty appetites we praise your name, O
God.

> Father bless our bread and meat,
> And those who work for us to eat,
> Make us strong that we may too
> Work for others and for you.
> Make us kind and glad to share
> With hungry people everywhere.
> Thank you, Father, for our food.
> Thank you, Lord, for all things good.[25]

Margaret Rose

For what we are about to receive, may the Lord make us truly
grateful.*

> All good gifts around us
> Are sent from heaven above;
> Then, thank the Lord, O thank the Lord,
> For all his love.

Matthias Claudius

> Be present at our table, Lord,
> Be here and everywhere adored,
> These creatures bless and grant that we
> May feast in paradise with thee.

J. Cennick

Praise God, from whom all blessings flow;
Praise Him, all creatures here below;
Praise Him above, ye heavenly host;
Praise Father, Son, and Holy Ghost.

Thomas Ken

To Father, Son, and Holy Ghost,
The God whom heaven and earth adore,
From men and from the angel host
Be praise and glory evermore.

William Kethe

From all that dwell below the skies,
Let the Creator's praise arise;
Let the Redeemer's name be sung
Through every land, by every tongue.

Eternal are thy mercies, Lord;
Eternal truth attends thy word.
Thy praise shall sound from shore to shore,
Till suns shall rise and set no more.

Isaac Watts

Glory be to the Father, and to the Son, and to the Holy Ghost;
As it was in the beginning, is now, and ever shall be, world
without end.[1]

Glory to our bounteous King!
Glory let creation sing:
Glory to the Father, Son,
And blest Spirit, Three in One.

Sir H. W. Baker

Index

Classrooms, 124, 134
Cleanliness, 72–3
Climbing, 77, 79
Clothes, 38, 81, 190
Clowns, 151
Clubs, 179
Coal, 117, 152, 156–7
Coastguards, 155
Cold weather, 6–7, 126
Collecting, 77
Colour (race), 63, 86–7, 122, 147
Colours, 25, 87
Comfort, 57, 86, 99, 115, 148, 167
Commonwealth Day, 116
Composers, 151
Computers, 81
Concert, 140
Confirmation, 174
Conscience, 105
Conscientious, 129
Conservation, 49, 50–1
Consideration, 62, 65
Contentment, 86, 123
Cookers, 81
Co-operation, 116
Councillors, 112, 113, 119
Counting blessings, 19
Country, 47, 89, 107, 109, 113, 153
Country Code, 47
Countryside, 38, 40, 47, 51
Courage, 12, 26, 92
Covetousness, 100
Crafts, 77, 130
Craftsmen, 151, 156
Creation, 17, 38, 41, 51, 182, 190, 194
Creator, 161, 182, 194
Creatures, 17, 37–9, 45–7, 50–1, 80
Cripples, (see Disabled)
Crotchety people, 63, 65
Cruelty, 51
Crying, 99
Cycling, 18, 19

Damage, 51, 125
Dancing, 18, 98, 130
Danger, 78–9, 142, 148, 153
Darkness, 27, 106, 182–4
Deafness, 19, 160, 164–5
Death, 69, 138, 166–7, 184
Decisions, 112–3, 139, 158

Demonstration, 115
Denial, 12
Dentists, 158–9
Despair, 106
Differences, 115, 117, 119, 146
Difficulties, 93, 103, 124, 126
Diligence, 137
Dinner ladies, 125, 138
Dirty jobs, 19, 152, 157
Disabled, 19, 35, 161–2, 164–5
Disappointment, 9, 101, 134
Disaster, 166, 167
Dislikes, 146
Disliking people, 88, 91, 146
Doctors, 68, 156, 158–9, 166–7
Doing good, 105, 160, 172
Doing one's best, 4, 132, 136
Doing right, 4, 105, 134
Doubts, 103, 174
Drawing, 83
Drivers, 75, 156
Dull jobs, 157
Dull morning, 53
Dumb, 164–5
Duties, 73, 109, 114

Ears, 56, 57, (164), 165
Earthquake, 167
Easter, 8, 12–13
Education, 112
  – Committee & Officers, 112, 139
Election, 113
Electrical equipment, 81
End of term, 127
End of year, 32
England, 33
Enjoyable things, 82–3, 101
Enjoyment, 8, 16, 82–3, 109
  – of work, 157
Entertainment, 18, 75
Envy, 59, 147
Epidemic, 68
Epiphany, 31
Equality, 147
Europe Day, 116
Evening, 199, 200–1
Everlasting life, 184
Everyday things, 80, 81, 84
Evil, 26, 33, 34
Example, 9, 34, 67, 109